Would You Believe

ALSO BY KEVIN DWARES

A Royal Crowning Achievement

Right Place, Right Time: The "TRUE" story of my life (at least in my own eyes) from October 28, 1955 through the present time! Part 1

Right Place, Right Time: The "TRUE" story of my life (at least in my own eyes) from October 28, 1955 through the present time! Part 2

Would You Believe

A LIFE WELL-LIVED

KEVIN DWARES

Would You Believe: A Life Well Lived

Produced and printed by Stillwater River Publications.

Visit our website at
www.StillwaterPress.com
for more information.

First Stillwater River Publications Edition.

ISBN: 978-1-968548-46-9

1 2 3 4 5 6 7 8 9 10
Written by Kevin Dwares.
Cover photograph by SERGEY / Adobe Stock.
Published by Stillwater River Publications,
West Warwick, RI, USA.

Dedicated to Barbara Gold Dwares, the love of my life.
NEED I SAY MORE?

Contents

Preface *xi*

Origin of Would You Believe
Sixty-nine plus years in the making xiii

Airplane Incidents
Bagels and Kidney Stone (2016) 1
Twilight Zone (2016) 3

Anti-Semitic
Throwing student down the stairs (1973) 6

Automobile
Speeding on Blackstone Blvd—Barbara pregnant (1983) 9

Bad Behaviors
Bear in Hotel (Bear with Me) (1992). 12
Egg-caper (2025) 14

Funny Stories That Happened to Me
Passing car in front (1973) 17
Ice Cream—Houston, Texas (1987) 19
Texas Toast—Houston, Texas (1987) 20
Work Van, Wrong Passengers (2010) 23
Rhode Island Credit Union—Ice Cream Caper (2020) 25
Depositing a check for Jake in wrong bank (2025) 27
Story # 1 27
Story # 2. 28

Health Issues
Claustrophobia (ongoing) 30
Suicide Hotline (1977) 34
Vision—Blurry (2020-present) 35
Barbara Partial and Medical Records (2023-present 2025) 36
Conclusion 42

A Matter of Perspective
Heart AFib (2024) 43
Teeth (2025) 45
Vertigo (2025) 46

Israel
Jake and Barbara in Tel Aviv (2005) 48
Beach—Iron Dome (2011) 50
Missiles (2011) 51
Jake—Explosives in Backpack Thrown on Bus (2012) 52

Maine / New Hampshire
Restaurant in Hampton, N.H. at lunch on a Monday afternoon...March 2025 54
The Ditty Box March 28, 2025 (Wells, Maine) 54
Whirlpool water above jets causes huge mess 2025—Ogunquit, Maine 57
Maine Thrift Stores (All 2025) 58
Bittersweet Home and Garden—Wells (2025) 58
Fabulous Find - Kittery (2025) 59
Safe Haven Humane Society - Wells (2025) 59
The Ditty Box Thrift Shop - Wells (2025). 60
Time and Again Consignment Shop - Wells (2025) 60
YCSA Thrift shop - York (Otis) 2025 60

Meeting Famous People

Admiral James Stockdale - LA Airport (1987). 62
Congressman Barney Frank on airplane from Wash DC (1990) 63
Mike Ditka and the Chicago Bears (2000) 65

Premonitions and Apparitions

Neal Dwares - Passing away (2024) 67
Barbara - Coworker (2025) 68
Other apparitions I see in the house (ongoing) 69

Tomato Capers

Cumberland, RI Restaurant (2025) 70
Waitress in Diner-Kittery, Maine (2025) 72

Women

Ada (1955-death) 73
Esther (1955- death) 74
Shirley (1955-death) 75
Barbara (1979- ongoing) 76

Would You Believe the Following Stories?

Max and Sleep Study and Duffel bag (1989) 77
Shot at close range (1989) 79
Jake and Stereo out the window (2005) 81
Jake- from sneaky drinker to superior and excellent bar tender and Banana whisky in basement (2006) 84
Navy SEALs Overboard (2009) 86
CVS in Sanford, Maine - No bathroom (2025). 88

Wrong Place Wrong Time

Hostess Snoballs in Supermarket (1972) 90
Tweet Balzano's Family Restaurant (1973) 92
Kevin arrested cutting off firetruck (1975) 94

Dave's Bar and Grill (1998) 96
Woman at Whole Foods / Florida Hurricane (2022) 98
Sanford, Maine, and Deliverance (2025) 100
The Five Books of Moses and Kevin 102
My Eulogy (Written by Kevin Dean Dwares and read aloud at my funeral by my Rabbi) 104

Bonus Stories
About a Busy Time from July 2025-November 2025 109

The Spelling of the Word G-D **115**

Conclusion **116**

Acknowledgments *118*
About the Author *119*

Preface

I started writing this book on Tuesday, Feb 18, 2025, which is actually the 21st anniversary of our son Max Gold Dwares passing away. I didn't plan to begin this book on that day, but the world has plans for each and every one of us, so that date is fine for me.

I have been going to a mental health therapist for the last few months, which has helped me unpack some of the more complicated stories and has also helped me release some of the demons that I have held inside for many years. I thought that therapy wasn't worthwhile and, of course, wasn't a manly thing, but I have realized that this is far from the truth. It was and is helpful to me, and perhaps to you, the reader, should you ever avail yourself of the possibility.

I have named my fifth and current book *Would You Believe?* The title actually is something that I feel is quite apropos for me, since I have told many stories in my five books that I myself sometimes find it hard to believe.

It's hard to believe myself that in my life I have personally experienced many different types of incidents that ranged from airplane incidents, antisemitism, automobile accidents, bad behavior, egg capers, meeting famous people, premonitions, funny things, health issues, tension and terror in Israel, women giving me advice, being at the wrong place, and much, much more.

As you read my book, you will notice that I question myself and that I have some trouble believing stories that have occurred to me, hence the name of my book, "Would You Believe." The stories are all part of where I came from and have shaped me into the man I have become.

The reader may also enjoy the final two headings entitled "The Five Books of Moses" and "Kevin and my Eulogy."

I also finish with a bonus story about real-life issues that everyone has to deal with on a daily basis, as I do, and I have included these as well.

So, sit back and relax and buckle in as you begin to read additional short stories of my life.

As I begin to get older and mature (although some people would add the letters "(im)" before the word mature), I begin to realize that I am moving towards the twilight years of my life, so I may only be walking on G-D's green earth for another 100 years or so. I have begun to be somewhat forgetful and wonder if I will begin to experience dementia or Alzheimer's disease in the future.

Since I never went for serious counseling sessions, as my wife Barbara has suggested for many years, I have decided that writing is my therapy, so it's time that I tell all my stories while my thought processes and my faculties are still working. Hopefully, my stories will leave a legacy of who I am to the most important people in my life, namely my wife Barbara, my late son Max, my son Jake, my daughter-in-law Maria, and, of course, my favorite and only grandchild Maya. By telling my stories mainly for me, I hope that my loved ones and friends can truly understand who I am, where I came from, and where I am now in my life.

I decided, as I approach my 70th birthday, life seems to be in the fast-forward mode as opposed to the relaxing mode after working for 30-plus years, getting up at 4:30 in the morning to commute to Boston and then Newport as a thirty-year Federal employee. I thought by now I would be laying on the beach in Bermuda sipping nonalcoholic piña coladas, but now instead I am worried about many other things, as most of my older friends can relate to. I realize that many of my readers could give a crap about what bothers me, so since they couldn't care less, I will let them decide to read the stories or not. It is their call.

Origin of Would You Believe

Sixty-nine plus years in the making

For many years, I have always had dreams about my father passing away at the age of 40 on Feb 19, 1968. As many of you know, it may seem highly unlikely, but my late son Max Gold Dwares passed away at the young age of 20 on Feb 18, 2004, after battling Chronic Myelogenous Leukemia. Max's funeral was on the same day, Feb 19, that my dad died 36 years earlier. Is it a coincidence, or was it meant to be? We may never know unless G-D himself reveals secrets to us as we venture out of this earthy life into heaven or hell.

I decided to write this book that you are reading about stories of my life and what direction I took as I went from infant to teen to young adult, and now someone fast approaching the end of time, at least for me and people in and near my age bracket. We all go this route, and that, I believe, is the reason I wrote this book as my own roadmap of my life.

I had thought of numerous titles for my book, such as, *It Could Be Meant to Be*, *Right Place Right Time Part* 3, *the Conclusion,* and *Would You Believe*. I immediately eliminated all of them except "*Would You Believe*." When I read the stories about my own life, I also question myself and ask would I believe these stories if I were reading them about someone else. That's why and how I chose the name of my fifth book.

AND NOW BEGIN MY STORIES

Airplane Incidents

In the summer of 2016, I was headed to Israel to volunteer on a military base with the program called Sar-el. This was my 9th time visiting the country.

The Sar-El programs offer prospective volunteers an opportunity to live and work on Israel Defense Force bases to gain an insider view of Israel. Volunteers work alongside soldiers, base employees, and other volunteers, performing non-combat support duties such as packing medical supplies, checking and repairing machinery and equipment, as well as cleaning, painting, and maintaining bases. As you will see from the following two short stories, the program would end up being good for me since you will read my sense of humor and understand my maturity (or lack thereof) level. Both of the following two stories happened during my time traveling to and from Israel in the fall of 2016.

Bagels and Kidney Stone (2016)

A month or so before leaving for Israel, I had a kidney stone incident and a procedure as well to remove it. I was told by the doctor to drink plenty of liquid all the time to flush out my system, which I did. On the way to Israel, I was looking for my seat on the plane, and I was put in a row in the middle of two other passengers. I asked the passenger in the aisle seat if I could switch seats with him because I would probably have to get up many times in the night and go to the bathroom. He declined while telling me (and I quote), "That's your problem, buddy." Little did he realize that his lack of compassion and understanding would lead him to have a very bad night sleeping on the plane during the ten-hour flight from Newark Liberty International Airport to Ben Gurion Airport in Tel Aviv, Israel.

As I anticipated, what actually happened was all night long, I needed the bathroom, and repeatedly I had to wake the man up next to me to get up to go to the bathroom. A few times he mumbled under his breath, “fuck you, asshole,” referring to me.

I did try to tell him politely that I had a kidney stone issue, but he did not care. He finally said to me in no uncertain terms that I should drop dead.

I was a little annoyed at how he could speak to me, so the only thing I could do was think of ways to aggravate him. I even thought of ways I could throw him out of a moving airplane window, but I realized that was not possible. About 5:00 am, the stewardess came by with breakfast, and by this time, my two seatmates were fast asleep. When she asked what I wanted, I told her a bagel and cream cheese and tea for me, and since my two friends were asleep, I also ordered the same for them but also included a blueberry muffin for the asshole in the aisle seat next to me. I put the breakfast on each of their trays since they were sound asleep.

A few minutes later, I decided to take the bagels and muffin from the passenger to my right and put them in my carrier bag (well-hidden, of course). Somewhere around 5:30 am, the passenger on the left woke up and thanked me for ordering his snack. A few minutes went by, and the passenger on my left dozed off, and the idiot next to me was still asleep. The stewardess made her rounds and came by and took all the food trays away as the plane was about forty-five minutes away from landing in Israel.

At approximately 6:15 am, the passenger on my right woke up and realized he didn’t get breakfast. He pushed the button to alert the stewardess as he needed to speak with her. He angrily accused her of not bringing his food and demanded she do so immediately.

He was very mad and said she was lying. Luckily, just then, the pilot announced that the cabin crew should pick up all the food and for passengers to put up the trays and prepare for landing.

When we finally landed, the passenger next to me found one of his

friends seated in the aisle a few rows in front, and they had a conversation about how a passenger made up a story about kidney stones and that he was a fucking asshole. He was pointing to me, so obviously, he was talking about me. As we approached customs, the passenger turned towards me and told me to drop dead. As soon as I realized I was about to enter the customs line, I called out to him and said thank you for the bagels and muffins, to which he replied with the big middle finger. I guess the only thing I learned from that incident was I should have ordered extra bagels and muffins. Lol

Twilight Zone (2016)

Leaving Israel for the return flight home after volunteering at a military base in Tel Aviv was both exciting and sad. I was sad because I was leaving a group of men and women from all around the world who were volunteering at a military base, helping out those soldiers who were called up to do battle against the Hamas terrorists. I was also excited since I was going back home to see my wife and family.

A few weeks before my trip to Israel, I had watched an episode of the television show *The Twilight Zone* entitled "Nightmare at 20,000 Feet." It was about a passenger on a plane, played by William Shatner, who believes he sees a creature on the wing but is dismissed by others. The show was somewhat funny and scary. At the end of the episode, which I advise you all to watch, it shows the passenger being taken away and restrained, most likely to be sent to a mental hospital.

Well, I knew it wasn't the right thing to do, but I decided to play a joke on the passenger sitting next to the window. About an hour or so into the flight, I motioned to the woman next to me and asked her if she could please shut the window shade. She immediately did so, and a minute or so later, I asked her to open the window shade, and she did. I then said to her, "What's that on the wing?" She asked me what I was talking about. I said, "I see someone on the wing, and it looks like some type of monster." She said, "That's not even funny." I told her I wasn't being funny and I did see somebody on the wing, and she then decided to go to the bathroom.

A minute or so later, a well-dressed man came up to me, and he asked me to come to the front of the plane. At first, I said no, but he proceeded to say, "Do you see my gun and badge? I'm a federal air marshal, and you come with me now, or I will put you under arrest." I got up and followed him to the front of the plane. He explained that I was on the verge of committing a felony, a federal offense, by scaring a passenger. He went on to tell me if the passenger complained again, he would zip-tie my hands behind my back and bring me to the front of the aircraft and that I would be placed under arrest.

He returned me to my seat, and the woman was moved to first class. I didn't say another word to her for the rest of the flight until we landed back in New Jersey. As the woman walked off the plane, I told her that I really did see a man or creature on the wing, at which point she told me to drop dead. I told her to look up at the wing and see the (imaginary) bite marks. She did walk away, but at the last moment, she turned around to look at the underbelly of the plane as if she really may have thought a creature was riding atop the wing.

Did I learn anything from my ignorant and childlike prank? Probably not, but in the future, I most likely would not joke with anyone on an airplane or any other mode of transportation that receives federal funds, since I could have been arrested and charged with a felony.

Anti-Semitic

Throwing student down the stairs (1973)

While a student at the Providence Hebrew Day School in Providence, Rhode Island, from 1962 through 1973, I was always very unhappy with the education that I was receiving. From the first grade through the 9th grade, I was disillusioned. Even though I came from a strong and vibrant Jewish family, the religious studies at the day school were very rigid and strict. I didn't allow myself to fall into this type of education. A lot began to change for me when I turned 12, after my father died.

The school did not know how to deal with me and back then had no type of program in place for mental health issues, which I began to have. I became very rebellious and argumentative, and I wanted to leave the school badly. At the time, I decided to spite my family and everyone around me, so I applied to go to the local Catholic school to complete my high school education. At that time, the school said they were not allowing any Jewish students to attend. I applied to get accepted in grade 9 and again in grades 10-11. Each time I applied, they stated that the school was only for Catholic kids. I decided to ask an uncle of mine, who was an attorney, to sue the school on my behalf for racial discrimination. Since the school didn't want the negative publicity, they admitted me immediately, beginning the September school year 1972-1973. To put icing on the cake, they also gave me a full academic scholarship contingent upon me maintaining a B average, which of course I knew I could attain.

I was happy when I started the new school, but I didn't realize the can of worms that was about to open for me. On the very first day of school, everyone stood up to say what's called the Lord's Prayer, which I was unfamiliar with. The student next to me asked me why I didn't stand up, and when I told him I was Jewish, he said I was a piece of shit and told me that I was responsible for the death of Jesus. I said that's bullshit, and he said that he would meet me outside after school to kick my ass. To be perfectly honest, I was scared shitless but realized if I ran away from school like a little baby, the rest of my school year would be tough on me. I decided to take matters into my own hands and looked for every possible opportunity the rest of the day to exact my wrath on the antisemite.

Later that day, I was going down the hallway to one of my classes and had to pass a small staircase, and I saw my tormentor going towards it. Without thinking of any consequences or repercussions, I grabbed him from behind and pushed him down the stairs. I knew my number was up, so I decided I would strike first. I ran right to my classroom, and within a few minutes later, he came into the classroom with the school principal and accused me of pushing him, which I of course denied. Luckily for me, there were no cameras or cell phones back then, so he couldn't prove a thing. To make matters worse, would you believe at the end of the day when I was going to my locker, and again remember that this was my first day of school, this asshole had a locker directly next to me. He started giving me some shit and calling me Jewish names. The student next to me heard what was going on and said that his dad was

Jewish and he also was the captain of the wrestling team. He strongly advised that my tormentor better not bother me or he would get his ass kicked. The kid agreed to stop because he was afraid and, I guess, not too stupid. As a matter of fact, he and I actually became good friends probably for two reasons. One of which was he realized I was a nice kid, and most importantly, he knew the wrestling team would kick the living crap out of him if he ever bothered me again.

Automobile

Speeding on Blackstone Blvd—Barbara pregnant (1983)

Back in 1983, Barbara and I lived on Irving Ave on the East Side of Providence. Our street intersected with Blackstone Boulevard, which is lined with very expensive homes. We lived in our apartment from 1980 to 1985 before we bought our first home in Cranston, Rhode Island. Barbara was pregnant in 1983 and eventually gave birth to our first son, Max, on November 4th, 1983.

Before Max was born, I had a habit of speeding on Blackstone Boulevard and occasionally would get caught by the police, who would give me a ticket. I didn't really think about it too much back then that speeding was, and still is, reckless, dangerous, and stupid.

On one of these occasions, a motorcycle policeman pulled me over and gave me a ticket. I tried to explain to him that Barbara was pregnant and wasn't feeling good, and we were on the way to a coffee shop to get something to eat. However, he had already stopped me numerous times on the Boulevard, and this time he just gave me another ticket.

I began to think this was my third ticket in 3 months, and the judge told me last time he would suspend my license for a year if he saw me again in his courtroom.

So right after he handed me my ticket, I did what every normal husband and future father would do: I conjured up a plan in my head immediately to beat the charge.

I immediately drove to a small coffee shop in the Fox Point section of Providence and went inside and told the clerk I needed a glass of water for my wife to take her aspirin, as she had a bad headache and was pregnant. While I was there, I also paid for a few coffees and muffins for us to eat in the car and made sure I kept the receipt with me for future use.

Around a month or so later, I received a notice to appear in court on Harris Avenue in Providence for a court appearance.

When my name was called, I was told to approach the bench. The judge, who by then knew who I was, first said he was going to suspend my license for one year, as he promised to do before.

He asked me how I intended to plead to the charge of being a habitual speeder, and I said "Nolo," which means you're guilty with a reason.

When the judge asked me to explain my story, I told him that Barbara was pregnant and wasn't feeling well that day, so we were on the way to a coffee shop for a drink and muffins to calm her stomach. The judge asked if I could prove I went to the coffee shop that day. I said that I usually kept receipts for our budget, and I clumsily looked in my wallet and took out three or four receipts. It just so happened that I found the coffee shop receipt from the day the policeman pulled me over. The judge looked at my receipt and decided that since Barbara was pregnant, he dismissed the ticket as well as the court costs. He

did tell me, however, if I came before him again, my license would be suspended. I thanked him kindly and left the courthouse. The funny thing is that if the judge had thought about it, he would have realized that the policeman pulled me over and gave me a ticket less than a two-minute drive from our apartment. He would have realized that I was bullshitting him. I believe that he decided to let me off the hook one more time since Barbara was pregnant, and he also knew from my past traffic violations that I had all of my prior charges dismissed since my Uncle Joe was politically connected. I decided that day not to speed again on Blackstone Boulevard or anywhere else. I was lucky I could think of a quick scheme but decided my luck was running out, and it was time for me to grow up.

Bad Behaviors

Bear in Hotel (Bear with Me) (1992).

In 1992, Max was nine years old, and Jake had just turned two years old. Barbara and I decided to take a small family vacation to New Hampshire in the winter, as we enjoyed the location and the scenery. I can't recall now the name of the hotel since it was sold many years later and was turned into expensive condominiums.

"Bear with me," as I get to the story. We arrived in Bartlett, New Hampshire, to begin our family getaway. From doing some research, I had heard there had been numerous black bear sightings and incidents, with reports of bears breaking into cars, roaming yards, and even entering homes. There have also been reports of bears in the area becoming accustomed to human presence, even to the point of "no fear."

As we approached the hotel, the first thing we noticed were huge chains and padlocks on the outside trash containers. I didn't think much of it then but should have wondered why a trash container would be locked up.

The answer soon would be clear when I noticed that the front door of the hotel had metal doors and heavy-duty screens covering the front door. Did I mention there were teeth marks and huge scratches on the door as well?

I did begin to get a little concerned, and after parking our van and getting our luggage in, within a few minutes we were at the front desk checking in. The clerk was rather friendly, and when I asked him why there were large bite and scratch marks on the top of the check-in desk, he said that was the work of Louie, a black bear that would hang around the property. I asked him if there was anything else we needed to worry about, and he calmly mentioned that the hotel had an indoor/outdoor swimming pool, which meant when you were inside it was very warm, and you could swim underneath a plastic partition and you would end up being outside in the freezing cold weather.

He said at night the bear would occasionally come around the property, and on a few occasions, it would swim in the pool. We were advised not to go outside the pool at night and to only use the pool during the daytime, when the bear would mostly stay away.

You know Kevin (that's me) sometimes does stupid things, so one night Barbara and I took Max and Jake to the pool and noticed that no one was swimming. So I jumped in with Max to enjoy the water. We sat on piles of snow, and we made sure that no unwanted bear was outside. I thought for a moment that if a bear showed up and thought we were dinner, we could get out in a hurry and go inside. Turns out during our three- or four-day mini vacation, we never saw the bear. However, on a few nights we heard some growling noises outside and rattling of chains. We decided this would be the last time to visit New Hampshire in the winter months. I'm glad you beared with me when I told my story.

For some added fun facts for the reader, it is estimated that around 5,000 black bears live in New Hampshire at any given time. It is known

that black bear attacks in New Hampshire are extremely rare, and the last documented instance of a black bear killing a person was in 1784. While black bears are capable of causing harm, they typically avoid people and are more likely to retreat than attack. Most encounters are non-violent, and attacks are often defensive reactions to surprise encounters, even though it's best to avoid the bear before he or she would ever take a bite of a human being.

Egg-caper (2025)

As of the writing of this short story in April 2025, the cost of eggs has skyrocketed from $1.19 a dozen, to some stores now charging over $5.00 a dozen. Barbara heard from a friend that Trader Joe's was only charging $3.49 a dozen with a maximum of only one carton per customer. The news is constantly saying that the cause of the eggs being so expensive is due to bird flu, but the chickens that we eat are spared from the bird flu. The simple yet complicated answer is that egg-laying hens are more susceptible to disease outbreaks like avian flu, leading to significant culling and reduced supply, which drives up egg prices. Broiler chickens, raised for meat, are less affected by these outbreaks due to their shorter lifespan and different farming practices, resulting in a more stable supply of chicken. If you believe this explanation, then I will sell you as many eggs that you want for $0.01 each or $0.12 a dozen.

Now, to get back to the rest of my story. On Thursday, April 20, 2025, Barbara mentioned to me that she needed some shopping done at Market Basket in Warwick, and she wanted to stop by Trader Joe's as well to get some eggs on the way home since they had the cheapest price around. She didn't really care if I joined her since she knew that I hated to shop, but she needed me so we would be able to leave Trader Joe's with two dozen instead of one. Her plan was for us to both go into the store separately as to not let the store employees know that we were about to pull a heist as brazen as the Gardner Museum robbery in 1990. On March 18, 1990, two thieves disguised as police officers tricked security guards into letting them into Boston's Isabella Stewart Gardner Museum. The thieves handcuffed the guards and stole 13 artworks over the next hour, making off with an estimated $500 million in art. The stolen works included paintings by Rembrandt and Manet, five Degas sketches, and a Vermeer painting called *The Concert*, which is thought to be worth $250 million.

By the way, the artwork has never been recovered. Now to get on with the rest of my "egg-ce-llant" story. Barbara instructed me to take two shopping bags out of the trunk and put my hat and sunglasses on. I was instructed not to talk, nor acknowledge that I knew her, and I couldn't walk anywhere near her. As we entered the store, she proceeded to get a shopping cart and sent me over to the egg refrigerator. She then said to me publicly that she didn't know me and to get away from her. I proceeded to go to the refrigerator and found a dozen eggs, some brown and some white. I wasn't sure which one she wanted, so I went to find her and began to talk, and she once again shooed me away. I made an executive decision to buy the $3.49-a-dozen eggs and headed to the checkout line to pay and escape the store without being noticed for my egg caper. I approached the check-out line with one item in my hand, and I noticed a woman to the left of me with about 30 items. I asked her if she was in line, and when she saw that I had one item, she said she was ahead of me in line and she told me to get back to my place in line. I went to the next available checkout counter and put my eggs down and paid $3.49. I was lucky to escape the store without being noticed (lol). I pulled the brim of my hat down over my glasses so no one would notice me for the crime that I just committed. I waited in the car as instructed, and a few minutes later Barbara came out and opened up the back door, put the groceries in, and she said to take off in a hurry. She was joking, but we got out of the store without scrambling any eggs and headed out to Market Basket to shop and celebrate our victory. I hope you enjoyed my story about the bird caper. We were lucky to get away with two dozen eggs without being caught. This was the first and last time (hopefully) I would ever run **afoul** of the law again. I guess you could say that we flew the coop and clucked all the way home about our (egg) caper.

Funny Stories That Happened to Me

Passing car in front (1973)

Way back in 1973, I was 18 years old and didn't have a care in the world. I was young and dumb and living the life of leisure. I was about to begin Roger Williams University, located in Bristol, Rhode Island, to earn a degree in psychology. I did dumb things then, and I still occasionally do today. I wonder sometimes if the degree helped me with my thought process or not. Most likely it barely helped.

On one occasion, I was driving on Park Avenue in Cranston, heading to who knows where. I was close to a car in front that was going too slow for me. So, what did I do? I cut into the left-hand lane towards incoming traffic and passed the car in front, whose driver happened to be a policeman. I sped away as fast as I could and pulled into a parking lot that happened to have a phone booth (I hope that you remember what that was). I ran out of my car and went into the phone booth, picking up the receiver as if I was making a phone call. A minute or so later, the policeman pulled into the parking lot. He came to the phone booth and knocked on it with a small blackjack, telling me to get the hell out. I said something like, "Could you wait a minute? I'm making a phone call," to which he replied, "Get out right away, or I'll put you under arrest." I obliged him right away, and he asked me to come over to his car and give him my license and the registration for my vehicle. He said that since I was polite and somewhat funny, he wouldn't charge me with attempting to evade the police. He asked me why I passed the car and went through a red light, nearly causing a major traffic accident. I told him it was stupid, that I was going to visit somebody, and I wasn't thinking. He wrote me a well-deserved ticket, which, if I recall, was close to $85, which was a lot of money back then.

He explained I could pay it in the mail or have a court appearance before a judge in the future. He advised me to pay the ticket via mail, but I decided to attempt to have the charge dismissed, so I opted to go to traffic court.

Two weeks later I got a notice in the mail to go to the Harris Avenue district court in Providence for traffic violations. The day of my court date, I was clean-shaven and wore a nice suit with a shirt and tie and was extremely professional. I was the only person that dressed up in nice clothing besides the judge and the court sheriff. I was called in front of the room, and the judge asked me to tell my story and how I pleaded. I decided to do the right thing and tell him that I was guilty. When my name was called, he looked at me and said that he knew me from somewhere. He asked me to approach the bench, which I did. He asked me if my father was Bobby Dwares, to which I said yes. The judge said that my late dad was a friend of his, and he said he was going to be lenient on me as respect for my late father. He said he could have suspended my license for 6 months. Instead, he charged me $85 and sent me for driver's retraining, which was held at CCRI in Warwick, Rhode Island. He further said that if I did not successfully pass the class, which was for five Wednesday afternoons, I would have to return to his courtroom, and he would take my license away for a year. I thanked him, and I told him I learned my lesson. I successfully passed the class after watching videos of people who were decapitated during car accidents. I decided to slow myself down in life and while driving. It was a lesson and experience well worth taking to heart, which I did and still do every day.

Ice Cream—Houston, Texas (1987)

In the summer of 1987, I was in Houston attending a conference about new and updated weapon systems for the US military. The conference was in the hotel next to the very upscale Galleria mall. One evening after an event, I went with a few of my coworkers to a recommended restaurant that specializes in steak and great ice cream sundaes. As everyone who knows me knows, I am an ice cream-aholic who can easily sit down and devour, or let's say demolish, an entire half gallon in one sitting. After dinner, the waitress recommended that I try the jumbo sundae that included five scoops of ice cream, with any two sauces, whipping cream, and nuts. She asked if we had ever been to the restaurant before, and when I said I was from Rhode Island, she said that if I finished the sundae, it would be on the house. I eagerly took on the challenge. It started to get a little hot inside, so I unbuttoned a few buttons on my shirt. A few minutes went by, and the waitress came over and held my giant sundae on a tray over her head. As she approached the table, I noticed that the sundae began to slide on the tray, and you guessed it, the glass bowl holding the sundae began to fall over. The waitress tried to stop it and began to grab onto it. It was, however, too late. As she got close to me, the ice cream flew out of the dish, and two giant globs flew right onto my shirt and down towards my belly button. The waitress had a very frightened look on her face and began to cry. She started to call for a manager, and to make her feel less embarrassed and emotional, I stuck my hand down my shirt and took a bite of the ice cream and calmly said, "Best ice cream I've had today." The manager came over, and after hearing the story, he apologized and ignorantly began to chastise the waitress. Thinking as quickly as I could, I told the manager that it was my fault since I tried to grab the sundae as she approached the table. She knew that wasn't the truth, but I insisted that it was my fault, and the manager apologized to her for getting mad. She thanked me profusely and asked if I wanted anything else. The manager interjected and said that for the next week that I was in Houston, all

meals and desserts were on the house. He also told me to bring all of the clothes that I was wearing, and anything else that needed to be cleaned, to the cleaner next to the hotel, and they would be cleaned for free, as the restaurant would pick up the tab. As the manager walked away, the waitress apologized to me and thanked me for not getting her in trouble. She told me that anytime I returned to the restaurant, I should ask to be seated at one of her tables that she was responsible for. The next day, I brought all of the clothes to the cleaner, and they did a great job on getting the stains removed. Believe it or not, I only went back to the restaurant two times in the next week. I went once for lunch and once for dinner. Even though the manager comped my meals, I always gave the waitress a very generous tip. I will, however, admit I never did get another ice cream sundae, as I decided one sundae down the shirt was enough for me to handle. Believe me or not.

Texas Toast—Houston, Texas (1987)

In the late summer of 1987, while in Houston, Texas, on a work trip, I decided to take an afternoon off to visit my cousin Steve, who was a senior engineer with the Houston Light and Power Company. My cousin picked me up at the airport. The average daily temperature in August is 84°F. When I went outside to get into his car, I took a gulp of air, and it felt like my lungs were on fire. Steve told me you get used to it after living in Texas for a few years. The first thing I said to myself was, "This weather sucks." We drove to his city called Sugar Land, about twenty miles away. His development had some very beautiful homes, and the prices were a little less than back here in Rhode Island.

One of the first things I noticed was that Steve had his washer and dryer in the garage. I asked him why he didn't keep them in the basement, and he explained many homes in Texas were on a slab and didn't have basements. He explained that Texas houses are often built on slabs (concrete foundations on the ground) instead of basements due to a combination of factors, including soil conditions, climate, and construction costs. Basements are less common in Texas than in colder regions because the frost line is shallow, and the soil tends to be expansive and prone to water issues, making basement construction challenging and expensive. Another peculiarity was that since it was extremely hot in August, my cousin would cut the grass at 4:00 a.m. or at 10:00 p.m. I thought he was joking until the next morning at 4:00 a.m., I was woken up by his loud lawnmower. Boy, was I pissed off, but I was polite because I was his guest. While I was there, we did a lot of nice things. We went to the Galleria Mall in Houston, which had a chandelier the size of my house. We also went to the space center located in Houston and saw some really cool items related to the space program.

As Texas is known for steak, my cousin decided to take me to a restaurant, and he further explained the history of steak. In Texas, steak is a testament to the state's deep-rooted connection to cattle ranching, cowboy culture, and culinary innovation. From the early days of open-fire cooking to the modern-day Texas steakhouse, the Lone Star State has played a pivotal role in shaping the way Americans enjoy beef. We went to a favorite steak house that my cousin enjoyed, and he told me that he went to the restaurant at least a few times a month. To be honest with you, the waiters and waitresses seemed to be very slow according to New England standards, as they were taking their time jabbering and bullshitting with each other. I was about to motion to a waitress to come over, but my cousin said this is considered rude in Texas, and they'll come over when they're good and ready.

The waitress finally arrived and asked me right away if I'd been there before. I indicated no, and she asked where I was from. I said Rhode Island, to which she replied, "What Island, and where is it located?" I had to repeat it. She said she knew I lived near Boston, as she and my cousin were friends, and she said she was only pulling my leg.

She asked me what type of steak I liked, and when I said I'm really not a big steak guy, she said a ribeye would be good for me to try.

After she took mine and my cousin's order, she left our table, and all of a sudden, she started ringing a bell. As she was ringing the bell, she pointed in my direction and yelled, "Virgin!"

She came over and said since I'd never been to the restaurant before, I had to ride the bucking bull, which was mechanical. I was watched by everyone there, and, you know, two seconds later I was flat on my ass. She laughed a little and helped me up.

She asked me if I wanted some toast with my steak, to which I replied, "Of course not, I only eat toast with peanut butter and jelly or for breakfast." She replied that everybody in Texas likes toast, and she asked me two or three more times. As I tried to say no thank you again, my cousin said that I was being rude and the waitress was being hospitable and wanted me to try a new gourmet item on the menu. I finally said, "Okay, I'll try a piece of toast," to which she just said, "Why don't you get three or four pieces?" I finally relented so she would go away. My cousin had his very funny face on, as if he was laughing, but he didn't tell me anything about it, so I didn't ask. In 10 minutes or so, the waitress came back with a tray above her head, which looked like mini loaves of bread. She put the platter in front of me to enjoy the toast. I told her I didn't want anything else, and she and my cousin burst out into stitches and laughed and laughed and high-fived each other, and then I realized they set me up to be made fun of.

The waitress said they do it to everybody who's new in town, and I didn't have to pay for the bread, or as they called it, Texas toast.

She further explained it in detail, and it was actually on the back of my menu, and I'll paraphrase below.

Texas toast is thick-cut white bread that's typically twice as thick as regular sandwich bread, giving it a hearty bite and a satisfying crunch. The bread is buttered on both sides and then grilled or broiled until it's golden brown. The result is a crispy exterior and a soft, slightly moist interior.

The extra thickness helps Texas toast have greater moisture and softness than what you get from regular-sized slices of bread.

Texas toast is often served with barbecue, ribs, and other grilled meats. It can also be used to make French toast, garlic bread, or grilled cheese sandwiches.

To be quite honest, the toast was excellent. Even though it was on the house, I was barely able to eat 1 ½ slices. The steak itself was excellent and very tasty. It was perfectly seasoned and well worth the price. The entire dinner and the company were great, and me being the brunt of a joke was all in good taste.

One final note to my story. Everyone except for me was wearing a cowboy hat, and many people had firearms as well. I almost thought with so many people wearing cowboy hats and guns that I was part of an episode of "The Rifleman" or in the movie "Wyatt Earp."

The funny thing was I wasn't in any TV or movie show. This was reality, and this was Texas, and you can now call me J.R. Ewing from the Dallas TV series. And be safe out there, y'all.

Work Van, Wrong Passengers (2010)

In the summer of 2010, I was working at the United States Naval War College (NWC) in Newport, RI. Little did I know that in four short years I'd be retired and living the dream, and not have to endure the usual bustle of commuting to and from work every day. From 2009 until 2014, I was part of a van pool that took anywhere from 10 to 15 passengers from stops in Cranston, Warwick, and North Kingston to three or four stops on the Newport Naval Complex. Eight of the passengers were drivers and alternated driving. The driver could keep the van at home if they chose but would have to be at the first pick up spot, which would leave every morning at 6:10 a.m. sharp, and then pick up the passengers for the return ride home beginning at 3:30 p.m. On a warm day, I was driving Van #13, and I began to pick up passengers and return them back to their vehicles at the public parking spots along the way. As usual, I went to the first two stops to pick up anybody who was coming home that day and stopped at the third stop. We generally waited five or so minutes at each stop for them to get on board. On this particular day, I made my stops and then put the radio on quietly since a lot of the passengers would sleep on the way home from work. I made my usual stops and dropped some people off, and then an hour or so later I was at my last stop of the day where I would leave the van that night for the next driver in the morning. As soon as I pulled into the parking lot in Warwick, I noticed three people getting off the very back of the van who didn't look at all familiar. I asked them who they were, and they said they live near Groton, Connecticut, and thought my van was going there that afternoon. I told them that they got on the wrong van as my van was #13, and they told me that they were supposed to get on van #23 instead.

I told them it was not my responsibility to see who everyone was on the van and that it was the responsibility of the passengers to make sure that they got on the correct van. At any given time, there were between five and eight vans coming daily to and from the Newport Naval complex, with a few coming from Rhode Island, Massachusetts, and some from Connecticut. Two of the passengers started to scream at me and demanded that I take them back to Groton immediately. They said it was a mere 50 miles or so, only an hour and a half with traffic, and an hour and a half back to Warwick. When I told them they were responsible to get the right van, they used a lot of language towards me and threatened to give me an ass whipping. Lucky for me, a police car pulled into the parking lot as they did every afternoon because of the occasional break-ins of vehicles left in the parking lot all day. I motioned to the policeman to come over, and he did, and he asked me what's going on. I told my story about them getting on the wrong van, and he told them it's their responsibility, not mine. Although the policeman agreed, he felt that I had some responsibility and that I should contact the van share company to see if they can be picked up. I agreed, and I called the company whose headquarters was in Connecticut. They agreed to send a van within the next few hours to pick them up. It was raining slightly, so the police officer said he would stay at the scene, and the three men could stay in his car until they were picked up.

After this incident, anytime I drove the commuter van, I always made sure I knew who was getting into the van. This is the end of the story of the wrong van but the right day.

Rhode Island Credit Union—Ice Cream Caper (2020)

We moved to our new home in Garden City in Cranston, Rhode Island, in Oct 2017. Our bank used to be located on Pontiac Ave but moved to its current location on Reservoir Ave shortly after we moved into our new house. Sometime in the summer of 2020, COVID was in full bloom, and masks were required to be worn everywhere. One day I needed to go to the bank to deposit a few checks and talk to the manager about getting a new ATM card. My old card had snapped in half in my wallet, probably from keeping it in my back pocket. Due to this happening and having some back aches, it was recommended to me by my PCP to no longer keep my wallet in my back pocket. I took this advice, and since 2020, I keep it in my front pocket of my pants and have had very few back aches since.

On the day of my story, I had a few errands to run and decided to first stop at a local market to buy a few half gallons of ice cream. My granddaughter, Maya, had planned to come over after school. It was fairly hot that day, so I put the ice cream in one of the cooler bags that I always kept in the hatch of the car. I stopped at the bank and made the assumption that I would only be in the bank for a short time. I entered the bank wearing my mask, and I sat and waited my turn, which seemed to take a long time even though it probably took five or so minutes at most. When it was my turn, I told the manager first that I had to go to my car to get something since it was getting very hot outside and that I would be back in a few minutes. I went outside and retrieved the bag which contained the two half gallons and put my mask back on with my hat and sunglasses and went back inside. The manager motioned me to come into her office, and immediately I sensed that she was getting a little nervous. When she asked what was in the bag, I told her ice cream. Maybe she thought I may have had a gun or a bomb. She asked me what was the purpose of my visit, and I told her to deposit two checks and to get a replacement for my broken ATM card. She said she would be back in a few minutes. I thought nothing of it until ten or so minutes went by, and I saw two policemen enter the bank and immediately come to the office door and told me to stand up and walk towards them. They told me to walk backwards with my arms raised high and asked what was in the bag. I told them ice cream and that I brought the bag inside the bank since it was hot outside. They looked in the bag and realized that I was telling the truth. They conversed with the manager and decided that I was no threat. The manager cashed my checks and processed my new ATM card request. She laughed a little

and asked me if I had any questions. When I said I wouldn't mind if she got me a few spoons to eat the ice cream, she replied if she did, she would get them. I left the bank and drove the five minutes or so home with my air conditioning on full speed. By luck, by the time I got home, I was able to salvage the ice cream and put it in the freezer. The next time I came to the bank, the manager and I had a good laugh about the "ice cream caper."

Depositing a check for Jake in wrong bank (2025)

They say money is the root of all evil, but besides that, it's also the cause of much aggravation at times. The following two short bank stories will illustrate what I mean.

Story # 1

A few years ago, I gave my son Jake a check for $34.00 to reimburse him for something he bought for me. I made the check out like I had done with other checks over the years. I dated it, wrote out his name, wrote out the actual dollar amount, and filled in the area with 34.00, and then signed it. I didn't think anything of it until a day or so later, when I was at home and my phone rang. It was the branch manager at my bank. She said that my son, Jake Dwares, had a check that I wrote for $34.00, but it also looked like it was written in the box area in the amount of $3400.00. She explained that the new optical reader at the bank read it as the higher amount. I told her it was for $34.00, and she said that to clear up the confusion, I should come to the bank and write out a new check. I told her that I was going on an errand and I would pick up the incorrect check. I called Jake and told him to forget about the check, and I would stop by his house later (which I did) with the cash.

Suffice it to say, it's a good thing my son is honest and didn't attempt to cash the check as it was written for the much higher amount. Easy come and (almost easy goes).

Story # 2.

In mid-February 2025, I sent an online check from my bank to my son Jake's bank account at Citizens Bank. I asked my son every few days if he had received the check, but he kept saying it hadn't arrived yet. Without telling Jake, I decided to walk to the Citizens Bank located in Garden City, Cranston, RI, to inquire about the check. I asked one of the tellers if the check had been deposited into Jake's account. I provided them with his bank account number along with my license to verify that we both had the same last name. The bank refused to give me any information, so I asked to talk to the manager. She told me that she couldn't provide me with any information unless my name was also on the bank account. She suggested that I go to Bank of America near the top of Sockanosset Road, just in case I had made a mistake and Jake's account was there. I thanked them and took the 20-minute walk to the bank. I arrived at the bank and asked them about the deposit, and they kindly told me that they had no account in the bank with the last name

of Dwares. I texted and called Jake, and he finally responded and said that Citizens Bank was his bank. I told Jake to check his bank account every day and let me know when the check arrived. A few days later, he told me the deposit was made into his account. It took nine days from the day I sent the check from my online bank to finally get deposited into Jake's account. I called my bank on Reservoir Ave and asked why it took nine days. They explained that a new "payee" added to my account can take a few days or longer, then three to four days more for the check to be sent to another bank, then a few additional days for the check to clear. I was asked by my bank why I didn't simply write a check and walk to Jake's account in Garden City and deposit it, thereby cutting the nine days down to two to three days. I could only respond with the words "I will next time" and quietly say to myself, "Duh."

Health Issues

Claustrophobia (ongoing)

Do you know what the word claustrophobia means? The technical term is "a phobia, or an irrational fear, of enclosed spaces." Individuals with claustrophobia experience intense anxiety and distress when they are in or anticipate being in confined environments, such as elevators or small rooms.

My claustrophobia can be a significant impairment in daily life, causing me to avoid situations that trigger their anxiety, like being in an elevator. I have personally been claustrophobic for more than 20 years, and it has been getting much worse lately.

My phobia began around 2005. I had gone downstairs on a Friday afternoon around 2:45 pm into the basement storage area in the building called Sims Hall I worked in as a federal employee. Sims Hall at the Naval War College in Newport was originally built as a barracks in 1904. It was later converted into a war-gaming center in the late 1950s. The basement in the building was old, damp, and musty, but that is where old files were kept for many years. For some reason that I can't recall, I needed to find an old folder or two dating back many years. It took me an hour or so to find it, but when I was done, my hands were filthy from dirt and grime. When I was done, I went down the hall and into a small, decrepit bathroom to wash my hands. It took a while to get them cleaned. I wiped off my hands and reached for the door handle to exit the bathroom. All of a sudden, I realized that the door lock was jammed and I couldn't open the door. I banged on the door, but no one heard me since very few people ever went into the basement. I tried to use my cellphone to call my office, but I forgot that cell phones didn't work since the building had jamming capabilities because it was considered a classified secret building. I banged and banged on the door but realized no one would know that I was missing until Barbara, my wife, would wonder why I wasn't home an hour or so after I left work, which was about 4:30 pm. I screamed and shouted like a crazed and caged maniac. I kicked and pounded at the door and tried to break a metal pipe from the sink to attempt to punch a hole in the door to no avail. I also smashed the mirror to get a piece of the metal frame off to try and use it as a key to try and open the lock again, to no use. I kicked and screamed until I was hoarse. I realized by then it was 5:30; I had been trapped close to 3 hours. I cried my lungs out and began to have very bad thoughts since the likelihood that I would be found were very slim since it was a Friday afternoon and generally everyone was gone by now for the weekend. I began to have trouble breathing and at one point, believe it or not, thought of cutting my wrists and falling asleep, slowly and permanently ending my nightmare. I said all types of prayers to G-d and others and thought about not seeing my wife and son Jake again. As you all know, my son Max passed away the year before in 2004, so I said a special prayer to him and asked him to talk to G-d on my behalf and get me out of the bathroom soon. Another hour or so went by, and I heard someone whistling in the basement down the hall.

I screamed and yelled and screamed and yelled, and finally I heard somebody say, "Where are you?" I kept screaming and said, "I'm down the hall in the bathroom near the old conference room." Within a minute or so, someone started banging on the door, and he said he thought he heard a noise in the building and went to explore. He told me he was a lieutenant commander working in the building for the weekend, and just by chance he heard some noises. He tried to open up the door, but he couldn't, so he decided to call security and the fire department. I was screaming and crying like a wounded animal, and I asked him if he could just blow a hole in the door handle with a shotgun. I must have been thinking of an old MacGyver television episode or Mission Impossible.

Within five minutes or so, I heard a few men come down the hallway and say they were from the naval fire department and that they would be using a machine similar to the jaws of life to cut open the door lock and the handle. They told me to turn around and take my sport jacket off and put it over my head so I would not get hit by all the metal debris soon to be flying around. It seemed like an eternity, but the next thing I knew, the door was open, and I hugged the three firemen and the military commander and told them that dinner was on me anytime to thank them for taking care of me and getting me out safely. They did mention to me that that bathroom door should have been locked permanently, as there were reports from other people that they were locked in it in the past. As soon as I got out of the building, I called Barbara and told her I was sorry I would be late and briefly told her my story. She said she tried calling me many times and thought maybe I had stopped on the way home for dinner with some friends.

As soon as I got home that night, I took a shower because I was drenched from sweat and fear. Since that day, anytime I'm in the bathroom or small rooms without windows, I feel very claustrophobic and begin to feel anxious, experience shakiness and sweating, and sometimes feel faint.

Since then, I have had numerous incidents involving me feeling extremely claustrophobic. The first was in 2016 when I was visiting friends in Beer Sheva, a southern town in Israel not far from the Gaza strip. Due to the occasional rocket terrorist attacks, most families have a safe room to be able to lock themselves in, in case of attack. These rooms have thick doors and heavy locks and generally no windows. I was given the safe room to sleep in. As soon as I heard the thick door slam shut, I had a panic attack and needed to prop the door open with a large box. I could now sleep in that room for the night.

The most recent incident occurred on April 14, 2025, when

Barbara needed to have an EKG prior to carpal and cubital surgery on April 24th. After her pre-op testing, we decided to go downstairs to the cafeteria, which is located in the basement. As soon as the elevator door slammed shut, I hugged Barbara tightly as I began to hyperventilate and almost cried out loud. As soon as the door opened, I ran out and gasped for air and asked a hospital employee for the nearest staircase. We then went over to the Ambulatory Care Center, and we scouted out all the possible elevators and staircases. I realized that there would be six possible elevators the day of her surgery. I went over the possible locations and times in my mind that I would have to go in an elevator and feel entombed. I thankfully was able to figure out where the staircases were located near all the elevators that day.

As of the writing of this story, I have been seeing a therapist who hopefully can help me address my claustrophobia and elevator phobias. And I am not ashamed to admit that even Kevin Dean Dwares needs "HELP." And now you read my story one room at a time.

Suicide Hotline (1977)

In 1977, I volunteered at a 24-hour suicide prevention hotline located at the Warwick Police Department headquarters in Warwick, Rhode Island. This volunteer position allowed me to fulfill a requirement for one of my college psychology classes at Rhode Island College. The training with other volunteers was held for an hour or so before my shift on the very first time I was set to volunteer. This consisted of the volunteer coordinator explaining how the telephone system worked and when to contact the police so they could listen in on phone calls if needed. We were told that if anyone ever called in threatening suicide, that call always took priority. I was told that was a rare occurrence, but it could happen during anyone's shift. On my first 4-hour shift from 5:00 - 9:00 pm, most of the phone calls I had were from people saying they were looking for a lost pet or had just broken up with a loved one. On these calls, we could refer the caller to one of many social service agencies who might be prepared to offer some advice or a point of contact. Approximately 5 minutes before I was to clock out for the night, the phone rang and the caller immediately told me that she had a gun and had also opened up many pill bottles and was preparing to swallow them all. I dialed the emergency police number to have them listen, and I tried to keep the caller on the line so the police could trace the phone call just in case it wasn't a hoax.

I tried to offer some help and attempted to defuse the situation at hand. My stomach was in knots, but I had some appreciation and understanding as to what was going on.

When the caller began to scream and shout and tell me that a loved one had died recently and that no one understood her pain, I told that caller that my uncle had committed suicide the day my father's shiva (Jewish period of mourning) ended back in 1968.

This seemed to calm the caller down somewhat, as I told her that medical help and police were on the way. She promised that she would stay on the phone with me if I did the same. Of course, I agreed, and within five or so minutes, I could hear that the police had arrived. The officer told me that they found a loaded gun along with many opened bottles of pills strewn all about the apartment. I told the caller that she was in good hands, and I wished her good luck and I would say a prayer for her complete recovery. She thanked me for staying on the phone with her. I never did hear of the outcome of her threatened suicide, but I hope in some small measure I was helpful in diffusing a bad situation.

It was a rough night volunteering, but I came back many times again to volunteer, although none of my calls were ever as serious and strenuous as the attempted suicide call that I had experienced that night.

Vision—Blurry (2020-present)

As many of you know, I had my thyroid removed due to a small cancerous nodule in 2005. I take Levothyroxine, a generic version of Synthroid, a prescription, man-made thyroid hormone that is used to treat a condition called hypothyroidism in adults and children, including infants. It is meant to replace a hormone that is usually made by your thyroid gland. One of the side effects that I have experienced over the years has been dry eye, which occurs when tears aren't able to provide adequate moisture. I have tried generic eye drops and punctal plugs, which are small devices inserted into the tiny openings (puncta) of the tear ducts in the upper and lower eyelids to help treat dry eyes. They work by blocking the natural drainage of tears, effectively conserving tears and eye drops, and keeping the eye moist for longer periods. The plugs are helpful but must be replaced (pain-free) every 3-6 months. I currently am taking cyclosporine prescription eye drops, which have greatly increased tears in my eyes, decreasing episodes of blurry vision. As told to me by my eye doctor, more and more people are getting dry eyes and blurry vision. She explained that the constant usage of cell phones, computers, and book reading from tablets, etc., is causing numerous eye problems, and a common side effect of this is

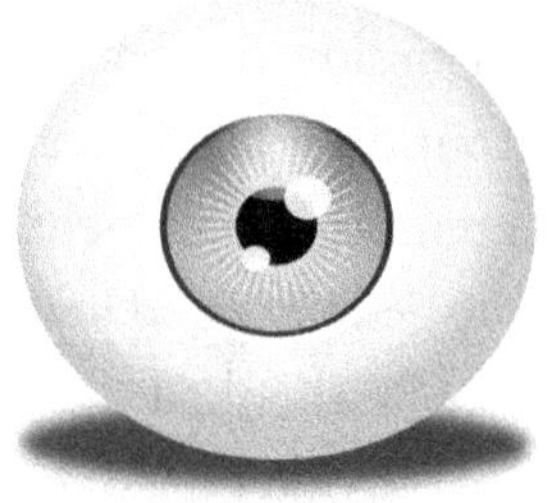

dry eyes. Reader beware, this may and probably will affect you as well in the future. So, in effect, technology, whether it be cell phones, tablets, or computers, may be helping mankind but also hurting the quality of life as well. Eye eye to you all.

Barbara Partial and Medical Records (2023-present 2025)

While the following story may not be of interest to many people, you may find some of it funny or simply far-fetched, but let me assure you that the story, which began on 06/16/2023, didn't end until 09/17/2025, or to be exact, 2 years, 3 months, 1 day, or a total of 824 days. It actually ended when Barbara had a new dental appliance in her mouth (called a partial) and that it fit, felt, and functioned properly for her mouth.

To hopefully help the readers and to have the story go smoothly, I will call Barbara's original dentist **CCD** and her current and much more professional dentist **CDA.**

What is a dental partial, you may ask? It is also known as a partial denture, and is a removable appliance used to replace one or more missing teeth. It's designed to fill the gaps left by missing teeth, improving both the appearance and functionality of the teeth.

During June of 2023, Barbara decided to get a new partial because her original two partials were getting old, and she was concerned that they could break or be misplaced. She made an appointment with her

(CCD) dentist to discuss it, take x-rays, and make molds of her teeth so a new partial could be ordered. What seemed like a simple task ended up taking an inordinate amount of time, and you will see why she ended up leaving her (CCD) dentist and found a new (CDA) dentist who would handle her dental work in a professional and courteous manner.

From the very start, the original (CCD) dental practice could do nothing correctly. Her office staff was constantly changing and totally inefficient. The dental practice had a lot of issues with getting our insurance approval for the partial, which began on June 16, 2023, and was finally approved on October 4, 2023. The actual dental work began during that time frame as well.

The partial came back from the laboratory that the (CCD) dentist sent it to, located in California, a month or so later, and it was not made properly. Rather than bore the reader with all the appointments and discussions, I will tell you that it never fit properly, and the dentist refused to send it back to the lab. At first, she told Barbara to wear it and see if she could get used to it. Barbara wore it for some time and returned to the dentist for many adjustments over time. Eventually, it broke, and it was returned to the (CCD) dentist, who finally sent it out to the lab. It came back, and once again, Barbara told the dentist that it wasn't fitting properly, but the dentist insisted Barbara wear it to get used to it. The day after she took it home, it broke, and it was returned to the dentist the next day. Barbara asked the dentist if she could use another laboratory, but for some unknown reason, the dentist always refused to do so.

Finally, on September 25, 2024, Barbara asked the (CCD) dentist to have the dental charge reversed to the dental insurance so she can go to another dentist and have that new dentist make a dental partial. The dentist refused, and until the day I am writing this story (**July 30, 2025**), she still has refused to reverse the charges, and this is where the story gets a little complicated, but I'll make it as simple as I possibly can.

In order to get charges reversed as if it never occurred, the (CCD) dentist who made the partial has to submit paperwork to our dental insurance program and also refund the monies that she has been paid. We also contacted the dental insurance carrier and requested that they require the dentist refund the money, but they refused to do so. They said that they paid for the denture and were not responsible for the incorrect and broken partial, as they weren't in the warranty business. This appeared to Barbara and myself as total bullshit since our dental insurance felt that the dentist should get paid for all of the work accomplished, whether good or bad.

I then, over the course of ten months from Sep 25, 2024, submitted grievances to FEP Dental (our dental insurance carrier) four different times, which were denied once again because they reiterated to me that they're not responsible for quality insurance if anything breaks, just if the work was done by the dentist. At this stage I was pissed off, so I decided to take another route and filed complaints with numerous federal and state agencies to get this resolved.

In the end, our dental insurance carrier finally relented and allowed a one-time exception for Barbara to go to another new dentist (CDA) to have the partial made, and my insurance would cover the cost, less our co-share. Unfortunately, the insurance company would not require the original (CCD) dentist to refund what they were paid. Then, after discussions with Barbara and with her agreement, we decided to stop filing grievances and sending faxes and emails, and making phone calls. It's hard to believe, but over the course of two years I wrote at least 200 emails, sent numerous faxes, had many, many phone calls, and received 30 plus letters and EOB (explanation of benefits) from our dental insurance carrier, and much more. The only thing missing was that it would have been nice if we saw white smoke coming from the roof of the insurance company, similar to what happens in Rome when a new Pope is elected.

Just to make a brief discussion, I will let you know who I discussed this issue with and tell you why the medical establishment, whether it be medical or dental, is just insane, ridiculous and simply a bunch of

bullshit. The consumer should come first, but in reality, this is usually never the case, and you'll see that the dental establishment, or perhaps just this (CCD) dentist, simply "sucks." For the sake of my sanity, and not to mention the dental practice, I am not mentioning her name for moral, legal and ethical reasons.

As I mentioned already, I contacted our dental insurance, Federal Employee Dental (FEP), many times to get the claim reversed so Barbara could go to another dentist. Our dental insurance denied our request, so I filed grievances with the insurance company, which were all denied. The rationalization given again was that the insurance pays a dental claim once the dentist has finished the work but can't and won't get involved with warranty issues with the dentist.

With Barbara's permission, I contacted the following agencies to try and get the dental partial charge reversed so she could get a new partial made at a new dentist. I won't go too deeply into our discussions with each of them and will simply summarize what occurred.

I need to, however, mention that I give total and 100% credit to Barbara for her one-line summaries that she felt summed up her thoughts and beliefs in each of the agencies that we dealt with. I will highlight her words in **bold letters,** and the rest of the words are mine.

ACLU: (American Civil Liberties Union) I called them, and they said to submit all documentation, and then they would decide to move forward. After much discussion, they said they most likely couldn't help, and we should pursue other avenues. **There might be liberty, but no justice was served. All we got was a simple message "to cease and desist."**

BBB (Better Business Bureau): They were extremely helpful, but in the end, after reviewing our request, they couldn't force or coerce the dentist to reply, so they simply closed out the case and said our complaint would stay on their website. **Could have been better.**

CCD: Barbara's original dentist **Needs a lot more practice and patients (patience).**

Dental Laboratory in Rhode Island: We visited this lab, and Barbara showed them her two older (original) partials. When the lab tech reviewed each appliance, he stated, "The older partials were made of high quality, and the new one in question was "inferior." **They felt that we would be biting off more than we could chew.**

Federal Employee Dental: **They finally got to the root of the matter but refused to demand and require the original dentist (CCD) refund what they were paid for an inferior product.**

Health and Human Services (HHS): **Filed a HIPPA complaint but still being reviewed and can take up to 18 months or more for a resolution.**

Legal firms: **They politely told us to cease and desist or else and refused to get involved and wouldn't sink their teeth in it.**

RI Attorney General office RI Department of health: Denied our request to investigate, so Kevin filed a Freedom of Information Request (FOIA) request for records, also denied. **In General, they could have been more cooperative in regards to this case.**

RI Dental Association: **Needs more practice in dealing with patients, which obviously they don't understand.**

U.S. Senator (Rhode Island): **Very official and by the book.**

OPM-Office of Personal Management. **They should learn to manage better and respond to requests in a more timely fashion.**

Finally, after contacting (or some would say harassing) all of the above organizations, our own dental insurance decided to make a one-time exception and approve a claim for a new dental partial. Generally, a new dental appliance is only allowed once every five years, so getting it approved was nothing short of a miracle, or more likely, they were fed up with my persistence, harassment, and badgering.

In the end, was it worth all the aggravation and time and effort writing hundreds, and I sincerely mean hundreds, of emails, many phone calls, faxes, and numerous complaint letters in writing and on various portals? Yes and no.

We may have won some battles, but we did not end up winning the war since we never could get the original (CCD) dentist to do the right thing, but still, what's right is right, and what's wrong is wrong.

While I won't recite the Hippocratic Oath, dentists in Rhode Island are expected to adhere to a code of ethical principles that guide their practice, and Barbara's original dentist did not.

In summary, the actions of the dental establishment and many, if not all, of the agencies that are in business to protect citizens failed Barbara Gold Dwares miserably. They all, in some fashion or another, told me that while their missions were to only suggest, but not require, dental and or medical professionals to do what's in the best interest of their patients, in reality, they simply follow rules and regulations but can't ever require the dentist to do anything. They simply can make a suggestion, but that's all.

It's up to the patient to fight for what is right. It's emotionally draining for everyone involved.

But the most important point here is that Barbara endured all of the pain and suffering, and in the end, all she got accomplished was having our dental insurance pay for a new partial, even though they fought us valiantly for many long months.

To those few who helped us along this often stressful and treacherous journey, I say thank you.

To everyone else who fought us tooth and nail, I hope that if G-d forbid someone going thru cancer or battling another horrific disease, and your insurance provider refuses to pay what is medically required, you will understand the pain and anguish that Barbara went thru.

Your love one could die from the ineffectiveness.

I leave you with these words.

It took a toll on Barbara and me to a much lesser extent, but in the end, we won. The system is set up not to help but to hinder. You should all be ashamed of yourselves, and I can only leave you with these fitting words: "**You Partially** know the story."

Conclusion

You can't do anything about the length of your life, but you can do something about its width and depth (author unknown).

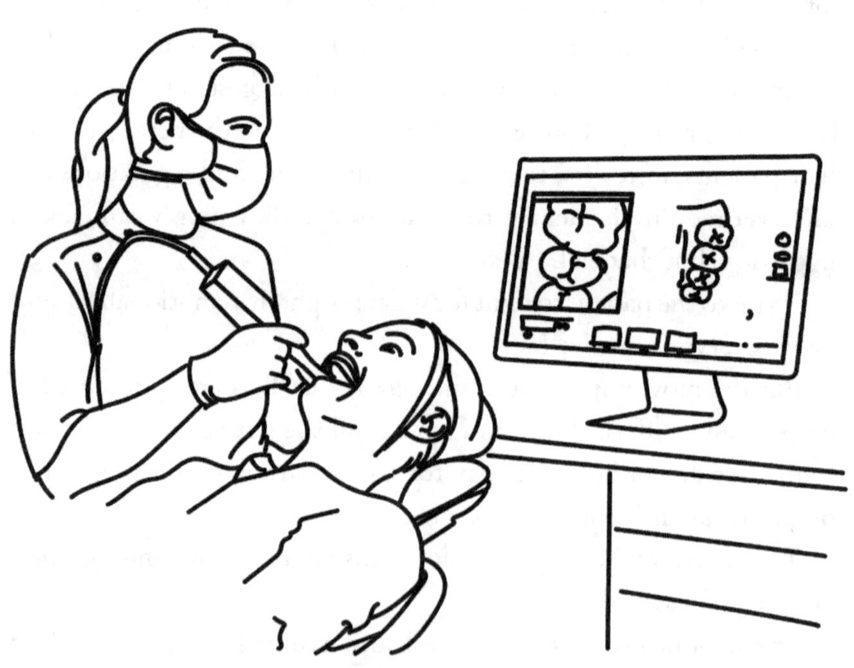

A Matter of Perspective

Heart AFib (2024)

On Tuesday, August 5, 2024, I was sleeping peacefully in bed and woke up around 2:15 a.m. with a stabbing pain on the right-hand side of my chest. I thought it might have been from something that I ate the night before, so I got out of bed and swigged down some Pepto-Bismol. An hour or so went by, and the pain got much worse, as if an elephant was standing on top of my chest, crushing me. I didn't want to wake Barbara up, who was sound asleep, so I decided to wait until 6:00 a.m. or so, when she usually awoke. I thought that I would wait, but about 10 minutes or so later, I was tossing and turning and decided I needed to wake her up to tell her what was going on. I told her that my chest was pounding and that I would call our primary care physician in the morning, and she said, "That's not happening," and she immediately called the ambulance. Since we live around the corner from the fire station, within 5 minutes, we saw very bright lights coming from the rescue vehicle, but no sirens. The next thing I saw was a fire truck, an ambulance, and a police car. The only thing missing was Del's lemonade truck.

Two of the rescue personnel came running up my front steps into the house and asked me if I was okay and if I could walk. I said yes, and before I knew it, I was in the back of the ambulance, where they immediately hooked me up to all types of IVs. Before any results came, they told me that it was most likely AFib, which is actually called atrial fibrillation.

Many people have heard the term AFib but don't really know what it means. It actually is an irregular, often rapid heart rate that commonly causes poor blood flow.

While in the ambulance, the technician taking care of me asked me many health-related questions and told me that my blood pressure was 180/130.

I was getting a little nervous, so I politely asked the attendant to shut the fuck up, to which he replied, “No fucking problem.” We arrived at Rhode Island Hospital in about 10 minutes, and I was immediately wheeled into the emergency room. They assessed my situation and brought me down to the cardiac area, and in 2 or so minutes, they hooked me up to two additional IVs, and then they gave me an EKG and then a stress echo. They then brought me to the sixth floor in the Bridge building at RI Hospital for cardiac patients to be monitored around the clock.

Over the next few days, I had blood taken every few hours and was told that if my heart didn't go back into sinus rhythm (sinus rhythm refers to the normal, regular electrical activity of the heart) by Thursday afternoon, I would be brought down to the cardiac surgical suite for a procedure. Just by luck, my heart began to function better. The cardiologist on duty informed me that I would have to take Eliquis to thin my blood so I wouldn't have a blood clot that could possibly travel to my brain and kill me, and Diltiazem for blood pressure. These would have to be taken for life. Before I left the hospital, I was assigned a cardiologist and made an appointment a few weeks later. Since Aug 2024, I have had a few further issues but pray that my good health will continue. I do, however, need to contact my cardiologist's office anytime I have a procedure which could result in bleeding, such as dental care, and the two medical professionals would discuss if I need to stop my Eliquis for a short period before the procedure. I would, of course, always defer to the cardiologist's decision. I was always told that I had a good heart as a person, but now I literally always hope to hear that expression, especially from my cardiologist.

Teeth (2025)

I know that in my home I am considered the king, at least in my own mind. I have had 21 dental crowns put in my mouth over the last few years. I detailed my dental saga in my book "A Royal Crown Achievement." I am sure that you probably are tired of hearing about all of my teeth stories, but the saga has continued through 2025. I was having pain again, and I went to the dentist who told me I needed another crown, this time on tooth 28. I had this done on Monday, April 28, 2025, and as of the writing of this story, I have no other issues with #28.

As you know, nothing ever seems simple with us humans, and of course, I had another dental incident not many months later. So as not to bore you, I will make a long story as short as possible.

On Friday, Aug 22, 2025, I had my dental cleaning (every 4 months per insurance), and the hygienist recommended that I use a water flosser to help eliminate or reduce food particles that can get trapped below the gum line that regular dental floss can't remove.

On Sunday, August 24, 2025, while eating oatmeal, for some unknown reason, crown #20 fell off. I contacted the on-call dentist, and it was recommended that I put on temporary dental cement until I saw my dentist the very next day. I was mad as hell, but since Barbara and I were attending a picnic later on that day, I decided to keep my thoughts to myself.

On Monday, August 25, 2025, I went to my general dentist, who advised me that the crown could not be recemented and that I would need to see the oral surgeon down the hall for an evaluation.

I was scheduled for an appointment on Friday, September 5, 2025, as the office had an opening. I met with the oral surgeon, who gave me a head CT scan of my dental structure and told me that tooth #20 needed to be extracted soon, as infection could set in and cause more issues. He explained that I could have the tooth extracted and leave a gap in my smile (not advised) or have a dental implant put in. This would involve a lot of $$$$$ and a three-plus-month time frame.

He advised that I should begin the process in the next week or so and that I should also have general anesthesia, so I scheduled the surgery for Monday, September 8, 2025, at 8:35 a.m. sharp.

On Monday, I arrived early, and the first thing the office manager asked for was my CC information along with forms to fill out. After this was accomplished, I was brought into the surgical suite, and a few minutes later, the next thing I knew, I was waking up around 1 ½ hours later with a titanium screw implanted in my jaw bone. The next process was for me to have a two-week follow-up, which I had on Monday, September 22, 2025, at 12:30 p.m., and was told that I had to wait three months for the general dentist to prepare a crown to be screwed onto the abutment and screw in my mouth, and hopefully that will be the end of the story for tooth #20.

After a few additional appointments, the final process began on Thursday, December 4, 2025, when the general dentist took impressions of #20 and scheduled the final appointment for Monday, December 29, 2025, to complete the final process with the installation of the crown attached to the dental implant.

I have had so many crowns in the last few years that instead of a prince, I should be a king.

I'm sorry if I bit off more than I can chew with another dental issue, and you can take a bite out of that.

Vertigo (2025)

Around two weeks or so after the dental implant process began, I started getting very dizzy, and my head was hurting. I contacted the oral surgeon, and he said I most likely was having some spinning or dizziness sensations called vertigo. This can be caused by vibrations and pressure caused by the dental work. What probably happened was that calcium crystals in my ear were dislodged. He recommended that I go to a physical therapist (PT).

I scheduled an appointment, and the specialist performed the Epley maneuver, who, through various head and neck movements, guided the crystals back into place in my ear, eliminating the vertigo.

It's a good thing that all the dizziness went away because the next step would have been for me to find a "spin doctor" or a "shrink," but they may not have taken my insurance (lol).

Israel

Jake and Barbara in Tel Aviv (2005)

When Jake was 15 years old, Barbara decided to take him on a two-week vacation to Israel to visit some friends and do some sightseeing. I was all in favor of it. Jake was your typical teenager, and getting away from everything would be a break for him and for me as well-not that I didn't then, and even today, still love him.

Barbara had already been to Israel many times, and she usually stayed with her college roommate, Sheryl Marks Ishai, and also visited her cousin Mira. During her visit, she also took many day trips around the country either via cab or train. Occasionally, her cousin or friends drove their cars; with the cost of gas hovering around $8.00 a gallon, they mostly took public transportation.

Barbara and Jake both had American rental cell phones with an Israeli phone plan, which allowed them to make calls to the US at a dramatically lower rate of .13 cents a minute versus using our US cell phone rate of $1.39 a minute, but remember that was 20 years ago.

On one of their day trips, Barbara and Jake both went to Tel Aviv to go to the shuk. In Tel Aviv, a "shuk" refers to a vibrant and bustling outdoor market. The most famous shuk in Tel Aviv is Shuk HaCarmel, also known as Carmel Market. This market is a major attraction for tourists and locals alike, offering a wide array of goods, including fresh produce, spices, clothing, electronics, and various food options.

It's a great place to eat and shop and, of course, go for lunch at a kosher restaurant called "Burger King," and I recall a small McDonald's.

On one of the days, Jake called me from Israel at around 11:30 am Israel time, which is 4:30 am Cranston, Rhode Island time. Obviously, he woke me up, and I was startled.

Jake had a most important question to ask me: "Where is Mom?"

To what I must have replied, "How the hell do I know? Aren't you both in Israel?" I asked.

He said he can't find "Mom," also known as Barbara. I asked him if he tried to call her, to which he replied yes, but he said she didn't pick up the phone.

When I asked where exactly he was, he mentioned the name of a few stores that both he and Barbara were familiar with. I told him to hold on, and I would call Barbara from our house phone (land line).

I called Barbara, and she was also startled. Since I called her, she asked me if everything was okay, to which I immediately said yes. I told her Jake was on the other phone and couldn't find her.

With the scene out of a Three Stooges skit, with my cell phone next to my left ear and the house phone next to my right ear, I was talking to both of them at the same time and then communicating back and forth. I told Jake to go out of the shuk and go to the street at the top of the shuk where there was a McDonald's, I believe. I told Barbara the same thing, and I told them both I would stay on both my phones until they found one another. A few minutes went by, and I heard Jake loudly say, "Mom." Jake then said, "I'm going to find you, and why didn't you answer the phone?" to which she replied, "I didn't hear a ring." Now they had found one another. I gently, poetically, and diplomatically said

to both of them that I needed to go back to sleep since it was 4:30 in the morning U.S. time. They both replied, "Thank you and good night."

I told him to enjoy their time and make sure that the volume on their phones was always on loud, just in case. To this day, some 20 years later, I still always tell Barbara to keep her ringers on her cell phone on loud since she has a habit of always shutting them off at night, when she goes places, or when she goes to work.

Beach—Iron Dome (2011)

During my visit to Israel with Jake, Maria, and Maya during the fall of 2011, Maria, Maya, and I would take a lot of walks to the beach. Jake was living in a town called Bat Yam, a suburb of Tel Aviv. The beach was a 15-minute walk at most from their apartment. During my time in Israel, the terrorist group Hamas would fire missiles towards Israel on an almost daily occurrence.

On one of the walks we took at night, it was very pleasant until we saw missiles lighting up the night sky. While walking, we suddenly heard a loud siren, and everyone, including us, looked up. From one side, presumably the Gaza strip, we saw 8 or 10 bright flashes moving at a high speed towards Tel Aviv, and from the other side, we saw bright flashes of light, presumably the Iron Dome missile system, which is designed to intercept short-range rockets and mortars, primarily from hostile groups like Hamas, within a limited range.

While it looked like a Fourth of July fireworks display, in reality, it was pretty scary since, on some occasions, people died. There is not much to say about this incident except that Jake told me that most people simply get used to the constant threat of terror and the possibility of a wide-ranging war breaking out at any time. I don't think it's a great way to raise a family, but as many Israelis like to say when asked why they don't move somewhere else, their general response is, "There's nowhere else to go."

Missiles (2011)

On another one of my trips to Israel in 2011, I was visiting my son, Maria, and their daughter, Maya, in Israel. Jake had been living there for almost two years. They eventually came back to the U.S. in November 2012. On the day that I arrived, I made plans to immediately take a cab from the Tel Aviv airport to his apartment in Bat Yam, a suburb approximately eight miles south. As soon as I arrived, I told the cab driver to wait for a few minutes so I could go into the apartment to get them. We were off a few minutes later on the way to the restaurant that Jake worked in, in Tel Aviv. Even though it wasn't a great distance away, it took a while to get there due to the traffic. I couldn't wait to see Jake and hug and kiss him, and since he is much taller than me, he would always kiss the top of my head.

When I arrived at the restaurant Jake worked at, there were many people sitting at the outside tables smoking, drinking coffee, and eating. We took a seat at a table and waited for Jake to come outside to welcome us. Within five seconds of us seating, I heard a very loud siren sound, and everyone got up from their tables, both outside and inside, and all cowered in the corners of the restaurant and covered their heads. In a few seconds, we heard a tremendous loud boom. Jake explained that it was the US-made Patriot missile system, which is designed to intercept longer-range ballistic missiles, cruise missiles, and even aircraft. It is mostly used to shut down incoming missiles. Ten seconds later, everyone got up and went back to the tables and began to smoke, drink coffee, and eat again as if nothing had happened.

Jake calmly told me that was the thirteenth missile shot toward Tel Aviv that month. He said it was just another incident in a long line of incidents that had befallen Israel and probably would continue for years to come. Jake was extremely calm during this incident and only minimally told me what was going on in Israel every day. He didn't want to get me worried.

Little did anyone know that a mere 14 years later another war would start in the Middle East between Israel and their arch-enemy Iran, killing many thousands of people, both Jews and Arabs, and bringing the warring parties close to World War Three. As of the writing of this short story on August 30, 2025, both sides have a very fragile ceasefire, but I doubt it will last.

Thank G-D that the greatest country in the world, which of course is the United States of America, an ally of Israel, is always on their side during this extremely volatile time frame in the world.

Jake—Explosives in Backpack Thrown on Bus (2012)

The scariest part of Jake and his family's Israeli experience had to be in the fall of 2012 when they were planning on returning to the US. Jake would generally take a bus to and from work, and after this incident that I am writing about, he would never again get on a public bus. On the day of this story, Jake was leaving for work around 7 am and quietly shut the door behind him. I heard him say goodbye to everyone, and off he went. I rolled over in my bed and planned to go back to sleep for another hour or so. A few more minutes went by, and I could hear soft footsteps outside the door and then a key fumbling around and the door finally opening. I heard a light tap on the bedroom door that I was sleeping in during my visit. Jake asked me if I wanted to go to a little coffee shop around the corner. I asked if he would get in trouble taking the day off, and he responded that since he and his family were leaving Israel to move back to the US, his manager wouldn't care at all. Within 2-3 minutes I had my shirt, pants, and shoes on, and we were out the door. We arrived at the coffee shop around the corner, and it was bustling with patrons and many soldiers with their Uzi machine guns slung over their shoulders. This was common in Israel with both men and women serving in the military.

Approximately 2 or 3 minutes later, phones were ringing all through the coffee shop. I could see the pained look on all of their faces. Jake's phone rang as well, and his face turned white as a ghost. He told me, while holding back tears, that after his bus left the station, and two short stops later, a terrorist threw a backpack loaded with explosives into the bus, fully intending to kill and maim as many innocent passengers. Just by luck, or the grace of G-D, the backpack for some unknown reason failed to explode. The police and many other people nearby chased after the terrorist. We never learned if he was caught and neutralized. (In Israel, that generally means they shot the piece of shit to death.) In the next few weeks before Jake left Israel, he always took a cab to and from work. When he finally came back home to the US, which was in 2012 or more than 13 years ago, to the best of my knowledge, he has never again taken a bus. On a side note, when Jake finally got a job, it was at a law firm as a cyber security specialist. And the funny thing was, there was a public bus stop at the end of his street, a mere 2-minute walk, and it dropped off passengers directly in front of his building. He REFUSED to ever take a bus to work again under any circumstances.

Maine / New Hampshire

Restaurant in Hampton, N.H. at lunch on a Monday afternoon...March 2025

On the way home from our one-week trip to Ogunquit, Maine, this past March 2025, we stopped at a small place for lunch. It was part pizza place and part bar/lunch establishment. While ordering our food, which was an excellent steak and cheese sandwich, we listened to all the bar patrons discussing which alcoholic beverages were better and caused less of a hangover.

Most of the people seemed to be highly educated, and a few were nurses and a few were doctors as well. They said that

generally, lighter, clear alcoholic beverages tend to cause less severe hangovers compared to darker, more heavily distilled drinks. This is because lighter spirits like vodka, gin, and light rum often contain fewer congeners (byproducts of fermentation) that are believed to contribute to hangover symptoms. Since it is well known to all of my friends and relatives that I don't drink any alcoholic beverages, the discussion seemed meaningless to me. I will continue to enjoy a nice cold glass of ice water with the occasional diet coke. I learned that you can learn a lot from people who like to consume alcoholic beverages.

The Ditty Box March 28, 2025 (Wells, Maine) Man from Scotland

While spending a week in Ogunquit, Maine, my wife and I liked to frequent thrift stores and resale shops. One of our favorite places is the Ditty Box, which is only a few miles away in Wells, Maine. The last few times we visited, we had met a dapper-looking older gentleman named John who hailed from Scotland. We usually only exchanged a few words, but this time, for some unknown reason, he began to tell us a story, or should I say, **a real-life** love story.

He first told me that he was a friend of the well-known actress of television and theater. Her name was Sally Struthers, who was on the long-time hit television show "All in the Family." He explained that she came to Ogunquit every year to star in theater productions at the Ogunquit playhouse and that she reminded him of his late wife.

He then began to tell me a fascinating story of his late wife, Margaret. But first, he repeated to me at least five times that he was born in 1935, which would make him 90 years old. I think he must have suffered from dementia or Alzheimer's, but I showed him respect and listened to his story.

He asked me to accompany him outside to his car and then took out a small scrapbook, which included pictures of him and Sally Struthers and his wife of 65 years, Margaret. He went on to tell me that he had spent many years as a pilot in the Scottish Air Force. After retiring, he went to work at Rolls Royce, then transferred to Malden, Mass., in the United States of America, to work at a well-known defense contractor. He told me that he married his high school sweetheart, and they were together for 65 years until she passed away during COVID from lung cancer. He told me that he missed her so much and that he wanted to go to sleep and not wake up.

While he told me the story of his life and his relationship, it was slightly disjointed, but I was able to piece it together as he repeated parts five or six times. As a sign of respect to John and his late wife, Margaret, I am telling his story in and out of order, but I am sure that you, the reader, will be able to follow along.

John had sat next to Margaret in school for three years in Scotland but never had the courage to talk to her. He joined the Scottish military and loved to fly planes, so he was assigned to the Air Force command. While he was overseas in a few countries, his mother would send him newspaper clippings about things that were happening back at home so he wouldn't get homesick.

In one letter his mother sent him was a newspaper clipping that had a picture of his graduation class. One of the pictures was of his old classmate Margaret. He asked his mother to get her address. When she finally was able to get her location, she sent it to him. He wrote her a letter, which took two weeks to arrive because this was the end of the Korean War. He said he was going to be home on leave the next month on a certain date and asked her to meet him at a local ice cream parlor. They met and fell in love again, and you know what happened: they got married six months later. During their 65-year marriage, they had two children, five grandchildren, and ten great-grandchildren. As I mentioned earlier in my story, John felt that he would have better career opportunities, and when an opening came up in the United States, he jumped at the opportunity. So now you know the story of John and his late wife, Margaret, and their wonderful marriage.

I obviously never had the luck to meet Margaret. If I ever did, I would tell her how much her husband John cared for her and cherished the time he spent in love.

Whirlpool water above jets causes huge mess 2025—Ogunquit, Maine

Twice a year, Barbara and I go to Maine and stay at our favorite place, the Inn Seasons Resort Falls at Ogunquit. We go to a lot of resale shops, go to the beach, go fishing, and take walks around the town. We enjoy going out to dinner, and by the end of our long day, Barbara usually likes to take a hot tub that also has built-in whirlpool jets.

Barbara thoroughly enjoys it, and she tells me that it is quite relaxing. On our last visit in March 2025, I began to fill up the whirlpool with water and also included a small amount (or so I thought) of bath soap for a bubble effect.

I need to mention that the whirlpool was in a corner of the bedroom and not in a separate area, which makes the story all the much funnier.

About five minutes later, I went back to check on the height of the water in the tub and decided that I would put on the jets to get the water to splash around with bubbles. Not thinking or realizing the water had to be above the jets, they began to ferociously send water and bubbles all along the room. The water shot up to the ceiling, causing a small flood similar to Noah's Ark. It was like a scene reminiscent of the movie "The Perfect Storm."

I began to panic. At first, I didn't know what to do. I realized that I needed to shut off the wall timer switch that controlled everything. In the minute or so that it took me to shut it off, the area in and around the room was soaked and partially flooded. We grabbed as many towels as we could find and began to soak up the watery mess in the room. By the time we were done, we had used approximately 10 towels, which were soaked. I wrung them all out and left them outside the door of our room for the cleaning staff to pick up in the morning. I went down to the front desk office and told them what happened, and the young lady laughed a little and told me that we weren't the first, and most likely not the last, guests that this would happen to.

Did we learn a lesson from this? I would have to say yes, but the water incident is a story that we will tell for many years to come. I guess I can say it's just all water under the bridge, LOL.

Maine Thrift Stores (All 2025)

All of the following thrift stores were visited during the month of March 2025 while Barbara and I were staying in Ogunquit, Maine. Most of the shops were a short drive from our hotel.

Bittersweet Home and Garden—Wells (2025)

This is a very unique establishment and is currently located at 648 Post Rd, Wells, Maine 04090.

The store owner (proprietor) is a young lady by the name of Tracey Walz. After many years in retail, she opened her first shop, The Secret Garden, in 1999. She then purchased the Rte. One property in 2002 and changed the store name to Bittersweet Home and Garden. She is a talented artist who designs her own jewelry and crafts. She makes a lot of the items offered in her shop, but this is not a consignment shop at all! She buys from various artists and crafters and accepts very few items on consignment. This absolutely beautiful little shop has numerous art displays that are a real treat to look at. It's a great place for buying gifts, and most of the items are unique and artsy, and have very good prices.

Barbara and I always buy something from her store. On our last visit, she bought a few beautiful pairs of original handmade earrings, and we also bought a metal, hand-sculpted butterfly.

Stop by next time you're visiting Wells, Maine. I can assure you it's worth the visit.

Fabulous Find - Kittery (2025)

This thrift store has very unique items and also includes a used book section where husbands and significant others can sit and relax while their partners go shopping. My favorite part of the experience is that it has some very nice candy jars that one can enjoy while shopping. It's worth the visit if you prefer higher-end and higher-quality items.

Safe Haven Humane Society - Wells (2025)

This is one of our must-visits every time we visit Maine. This thrift shop also serves as a cat rescue center and has numerous enclosures throughout the store where visitors can interact with the pets. Safe Haven's mission is to provide sanctuary for abused, abandoned, and unwanted feline companion animals where they will experience compassion and healing. They promote humane treatment, responsible pet care, and the prevention of cruelty through example and education.

They also sell a lot of knick-knacks, and I found a few of my favorite books entitled "Chicken Soup for the Soul." All the staff here are volunteers and are truly lovers of cats. We also purchased a very old folding bridge table there that is approximately 45 years old.

If you're a lover of cats, then a visit to the Safe Haven Humane Society is well worth your trip. All the money used to purchase items here goes back to caring for all of the pets that hopefully will be placed in homes for adoption.

The Ditty Box Thrift Shop - Wells (2025).

This small thrift store has many different items for sale such as clothing, kitchen items, jewelry, household goods, games, puzzles, fabric, and also a free section with numerous miscellaneous items. The store is used as a major fundraiser for a local church, and its success is dependent on its volunteers.

Time and Again Consignment Shop - Wells (2025)

This consignment shop in Wells, Maine, is located across the parking lot from Bittersweet Home and Garden. It offers a unique shopping experience for those seeking quality second-hand items. The staff was extremely friendly and it is well worth a short visit.

YCSA Thrift shop - York (Otis) 2025

As many of you know, Barbara and I have a dog and a cat. The dog's name is Harry and the cat's name is Gaby. Barbara will constantly ask me about getting another dog and a cat. I always say no since I am not a pet lover. We have had many dogs and cats at the same time; some people could say we live in the zoo. "lol". Barbara will tell me that since we have one dog and one cat, they must be lonely and they need companionship.

When we have the dog and cat discussion, I tell Barbara that I am lonely sometimes and that I should be able to have a "Human" companion for me. For some unknown reason, she always replies, "I am not discussing this now, or ever. Too Bad!"

On the way home from Maine, we stopped at a thrift store in York, Maine. It was called the York Community Service Association thrift shop. This store benefits the local community of York.

Barbara was looking at knick-knacks and some clothes while I was walking around and being bored. I noticed a stuffed animal that looked like a pug. I said to myself, "Wow, I'll tell Barbara she can get another dog." I paid $5 for him, and we named him Otis. He is well-behaved, toilet trained, and sleeps 23 hours a day. He has become a great addition to our family.

I would recommend this type of pet adoption to everybody; after all, he never makes a mess, he eats nothing, and the veterinarian bills are always zero.

Woof Woof.

Meeting Famous People

Admiral James Stockdale - LA Airport (1987).

In Dec 1987, I was in California to attend a meeting in Oxnard, California, at the Point Mugu Naval Air Station, which was involved in the development and testing of Naval missile systems. The four-day conference went well, and I also enjoyed some relaxation time, and I drove up the Pacific Coast Highway towards Malibu Beach and other places. One night after work, I went back to the hotel room to relax and turn the television on. I noticed that a movie was beginning entitled, "In Love and War" (March 1987). It starred RI native James Woods. It was about James Bond Stockdale, who was the most senior naval officer held captive in Hanoi, North Vietnam, after his jet was shot down in North Vietnam on September 9, 1965. He was held a prisoner for close to seven and a half years before he was released. To be quite honest, I had met many released prisoners of war (POW) while an employee of the United States Department of Defense, but this movie was very graphic, and it touched a place in my heart that still resonates with me today. At the end of the movie, it showed a few pictures of the real Admiral during his military career.

Finally, after almost a week of work and fun in the sun, I was in the LA airport waiting for my return flight home to Rhode Island. Los Angeles airport (LAX) is very busy, so I decided to get there two hours before my scheduled flight. I was hungry and decided to find a little restaurant nearby that was not outrageously expensive. I went in, sat down, and ordered a burger, some fries, and a drink, and was enjoying myself while waiting for my flight to be announced for boarding. About a half an hour or so later, a well-dressed gentleman came in and was looking for a place to sit, since the restaurant was full. I got up and mentioned to him that there was an extra seat at my table and that he could feel free to join me if he wanted to, for which he was grateful. As we were eating our snack, we were chatting, and he was telling me about his military career, and I was telling him about my civilian career with the military. He introduced himself and told me he was James Bond Stockdale. I told him that I had watched a movie a few nights before about a POW with the same name. I looked at him without being too obvious, and he didn't look like the person that was shown in the movie that I had watched. I tried not to be too direct and embarrass myself, so I simply said, "You look just like the James Stockdale that was portrayed in the movie *In Love and War*." He immediately said it was him, and he took out his military ID and showed it to me. I said I was sorry to intrude upon his personal life, and he said he was more than happy to discuss it and how he survived as a prisoner in Vietnam for seven and a half years. He told me that he held no grudge or animosity towards the Vietnamese people and that he went on to have a long and distinguished career. The most ironic part of my story is that Admiral Stockdale served as president of the Naval War College from October 1977 until he retired from the navy in 1989, a place that I was employed at from 2000-2014. After my conversation with him, I began to realize that life can serve up many challenges and disappointments, and that it's how you live through the rough and bad times, as well as the good times, that's important. God bless the U.S.A. and our troops.

Congressman Barney Frank on airplane from Wash DC (1990)

Barney Frank was an American Democratic politician who served in the U.S. House of Representatives (1981-2013) and hailed from the state of Massachusetts. A Democrat, Frank served as chairman of the House Financial Services Committee from 2007 to 2011 and was a leading co-sponsor of the 2010 Dodd-Frank Act. The Dodd-Frank Act, officially the Dodd-Frank Wall Street Reform and Consumer Protection Act, is a US federal law enacted in 2010 that aims to regulate the financial industry and prevent future economic crises. It was a direct response to the 2008 financial crisis and sought to increase transparency, accountability, and oversight in the financial system. Frank was considered the most prominent gay politician in the United States during his time in Congress.

In 1990, I was in Washington, DC, at a meeting at the Federal Bureau of Investigation (FBI). Congressman Frank was also at the meeting, so we chatted for a while about my federal employment and that I was a resident of Rhode Island and he of Massachusetts. He gave me his business card and told me to contact his office anytime I needed his help. Would you believe the very next afternoon he would help me out?

I was at the airport in DC waiting to board my flight back to Rhode Island. I already had my boarding pass in my hand and was approaching the check-in counter. All of a sudden, the gate attendant came out and said the flight was overbooked and no one else could get on the plane. I explained that I had my boarding pass already, and the gate attendant said, "I'm sorry." A minute or two later, Congressman Frank walks by me. He looked at me and realized he remembered me from the day before. I said, "Congressman, I need your help, as you promised me the day before." I told him that the ticket taker wouldn't let me get on the plane. He asked me why, and I told him they said the flight was overbooked. He said to get next to him in line and he would get me on the plane immediately. After he chatted for a few minutes with the airline employee, another passenger had to depart the plane, and you guessed it, that became my seat. I asked the congressman what he told the employee, to which he replied that I was his executive assistant and that I always traveled with him on official U.S. Government business. I guess the expression that I have always heard is true: "It pays to have friends in high places." Indeed, it does.

Mike Ditka and the Chicago Bears (2000)

In 2000, I was in Chicago on a three-day business conference for the Department of Defense. I decided to extend my visit by a few days on my own time and expense.

I visited the Sears Tower and also drove by the Playboy Mansion in Chicago. I also had dinner at Ditka's, named after Michael Ditka, an American former professional football player and coach.

To be quite honest, I am not much of a sports enthusiast, but I decided to go there for dinner. I sat down, and a few minutes later, a rather large guy, about 6 ft 5 and 225 pounds, came over to my table and introduced himself to me. He said he was Mike Ditka, to which I replied, "I'm Kevin Dwares." He asked me if I was a fan of the Chicago Bears; I believe I said "no, since I am from New England," to which he replied that I must like the Patriots. We chatted for a while, and he told me that he was a great fan of clubs in New England, namely the Boston Celtics and the New England Patriots. The best part of my evening at his restaurant was when Coach Ditka told me that dinner was on the house.

Premonitions and Apparitions

Many of my readers of my prior four books know that I have written about seeing ghost-like apparitions and premonitions my entire life. The difference between a premonition and an apparition are two very different, yet similar, feelings. A premonition is a strong feeling that something is about to happen, especially something bad, while an apparition is a ghost or ghostlike image of a person. I also have seen people, and not images, after they have passed away. Some of the readers may think that I am making this up, when in fact, I am not. Even while I am writing this short story, I can sense and actually feel a sensation that someone or something is hovering around me.

Believe me or not, I saw my dad and my own son, Max, shortly after they passed away. These experiences, which I believe are more of an illusion than a hallucination, can be a healthy part of the grieving process of a loved one that has passed on to greener pastures.

Why do I keep seeing a person who has died? After someone dies, it's normal to see or hear them. Some people also report sensing the smell or warmth of someone close to them, or just feel a very strong sense of their presence. Sometimes these feelings can be very powerful.

I also predicted the actual date that my late brother passed away, and also when my wife Barbara's friend passed away.

I also saw an apparition-like person in my house the day after we visited Max at his resting place on Sunday, May 18, 2025. I was sitting in our den thinking about visiting Max that day and simply looked out into the hallway. A second or so later, I saw Max as if he was being beamed up, similar to what happened in the Star Trek television series starring Leonard Nimoy as "Spock."

To be quite honest, I felt happy and sad at the same time but was glad once again that I was able to see Max 21 years since he passed away. Rest in peace.

Neal Dwares - Passing away (2024)

My older brother, Neal, passed away on Feb 11, 2024, at the age of 69. Neal was the oldest of five children and was almost forced into becoming the leader of the pack when our dad died in 1968. He, however, didn't have that type of personality to take charge and help out. Unfortunately, or fortunately, I, being the second oldest, was thrust into being the leader of the pack and helping my mom raise my two younger sisters and one younger brother.

Neal was a complicated person, and, to be quite honest, always thought about himself first before anybody else. I didn't really get along with my brother. We had a lot of aggravation with him over the years. Like my father, who was a lifelong diabetic, Neal developed diabetes at age 13, and this bothered him tremendously.

In a lot of ways, he used his health issue as a crutch his whole life, and this, I believe, held him back from becoming the man that he could have become had he applied himself.

Exactly a week before Neal passed away, I had a dream and also saw a kind of ghostly shadow of him in the hallway from my kitchen down to our bedrooms. I clearly saw Neal in the hallway, and I believe now, after his passing, that he may have come back to apologize for the way he treated me over the years. As soon as I saw Neal, I told Barbara about it and also told her that I felt that he would only be alive for one more week. I will have to admit that I was clearly taken aback by my thoughts, but whether you believe it or not, he died exactly a week after I saw his apparition. Some people may say that I shouldn't have said anything negative about my late brother, but they didn't live and walk in my shoes. They didn't feel the stress and aggravation that Barbara

and I felt over the years. I can only say now that I hope my brother Neal rests in peace wherever he may be.

Barbara - Coworker (2025)

Barbara had a coworker who I will call Sarah, passed away on Jan 07, 2025, at the age of 79. She had some medical issues but had been doing well. A week or so before she passed, Barbara had made some plans to go out for dinner with her and another friend as soon as her late friend returned home from visiting her family down South.

A day prior to her passing, I was sitting in the kitchen and suddenly felt a short, cool breeze go by my neck. I looked up and saw an apparition-like person with long hair that resembled her friend. She turned towards me and Barbara and smiled so softly, and seemed to be saying goodbye. I told Barbara my story, and she believed me, as these types of occurrences had happened to her many times before. I asked Barbara if she had heard from her friend, and she said that she hadn't. The very next morning, Barbara got a text from her friend's cell phone number and thought that it was her friend. Instead, the text was from her friend's daughter telling Barbara that her friend had passed away the night before. Barbara began to cry uncontrollably and said she was very unhappy hearing about her friend.

Could it be that her friend did appear in my hallway as an apparition, or was it just a figment of my imagination? Who knows, but I truly believe that I did indeed see her the day she passed on.

Other apparitions I see in the house (ongoing)

For many years, I have seen ghost-like figures in my house, and as I have mentioned, I also have seen deceased persons in the flesh. I know it might seem farfetched since no one, perhaps except for G-D, can see those who have died. Perhaps I have a gift to be able to see and sometimes talk to those who have departed, or it may be a curse. I will leave it up to the reader to decide.

Tomato Capers

Cumberland, RI Restaurant (2025)

In early April 2025, Barbara and I met a few friends at a restaurant in Cumberland, RI. It has a reputation for fine Italian and Portuguese food. As always, due to my tomato and spice allergies, I asked the waiter numerous times if the dish that I ordered had any tomatoes, tomato products, or spices. I ordered Bitoque, which is a Portuguese steak dish topped with a fried egg and signature pan-sauce made of wine, garlic, and butter. Fried potatoes and white rice are served on the side. I asked the waiter three times, just to be safe, about any tomato products or spices, and he said emphatically not at all, but he would double-check with a chef. He came back a few minutes later and said there was nothing on the dish that would bother my rather sensitive palate. Everyone else ordered their food as well. Well, of course, you know what ended up happening. I took a bite of the steak, which did indeed look tasty, and immediately I felt the sensation that there had to be some type of spice on it, since my lips began to tingle and almost immediately my stomach was tossing and turning. The sauce had a very spicy taste. I called the waiter over and told him, and he said he would double-check in the kitchen to make sure there were no tomato products or spices in my dinner.

He came back a few minutes late and apologized, saying the chef told him that there were spices and they could not rule out any tomato-based spices on my steak. He then told me he would replace my dinner with something else, and the only thing on the menu that had no tomato or spice products was plain steak. I told him okay, and he put the order in for a plain steak dinner. By the time he brought me my new dinner, my friends and my wife had already finished eating. Oh, and because my stomach was upset, I had to go to the bathroom a few times, so I barely ate any of my steak dinner. To be honest with you, I couldn't wait to leave. When the bill came to the table, each of the couples got their own. I was flabbergasted to see on the bill that I was charged for two steak dinners: the one that I could not eat and the new one, which was much more expensive. Not wanting to embarrass myself or my friends, I excused myself to go to the men's room and instead went to the hostess station to ask to speak to the manager. She arrived a few minutes later and told me that she was also the owner of the restaurant. I told her what happened, and she apologized immensely and told me she would immediately remove the first meal from my bill. I asked her how the waiter didn't know or realize that the original steak had spices, and she simply replied that she would in the future make certain that the chefs are asked about spices if a customer states that they have an allergy to some products. No one seems to take my tomato and spice allergy seriously, and that is very sad indeed. I hope it doesn't take the death of a customer due to an allergy to wake up the food industry to the seriousness of allergies.

Waitress in Diner-Kittery, Maine (2025)

While in Maine in March 2025, we visited Ogunquit, York, Wells, Sanford, and Kittery, Maine. We always try to find a diner to experience an old-fashioned atmosphere and good food. It was recommended to us to try a small breakfast place in Kittery. We called them and found out that they were closing in the next half hour. We drove as quickly as possible while obeying the speed limits. We arrived to see a small, well-kept place, and we proceeded to go in. We went inside, and the waitress came over and introduced herself, and I, of course, told her a few times about my tomato and spice allergy. She said that she was very familiar with allergies, as she had a very strong allergy to all metals.

I asked her how, and she explained that yes, it is possible to be allergic to metal, and it's a relatively common occurrence. Metal allergies are often a type of allergic contact dermatitis, meaning the reaction is triggered by direct skin contact with a metal. The most common metal allergens include nickel, cobalt, and chromium but can also include the metals in shoes, clothes, and other items as well.

I ordered the special, which included three eggs, bacon, home fries, and toast. Barbara ordered a vegetarian omelet. You wouldn't believe it, but within 10 minutes, the waitress brought over our breakfast, and in the middle of my plate was a cup full of ketchup.

I called the waitress over and showed her the ketchup. She was very upset that a mistake had been made, and she immediately took away my food and put in a brand-new order, excluding ketchup.

She was extremely pleasant, and we joked about all of our allergies. We enjoyed the rest of the morning, and we decided that the next time we were back in Maine, we would go back to the great little breakfast place again.

Women

Ada (1955-death)

My grandmother Ada (Namerow) Dwares lived at 236 4th Street on Providence, RI's east side for close to 55 years. Nana Ada had a rough exterior but inside, had a warm heart. She was married to my grandfather Philip for many years, and he, to the best of my knowledge, never showed love or affection to me from the day I was born to the day he passed away. I had heard stories about his early and difficult life, so I guess that is why he couldn't and didn't show love and affection to me. Nana had a lot of friends and loved to go to Chelo's restaurant that is located on Silver Spring Street in Providence. She would dress up, with her hair done and her outfits of matching shoes and handbag. She would drive her car, pick up one of her 80-year-old girlfriends and go have lunch. Many times, my grandmother would tell me to come to her house, and then she would drive to the restaurant. When she arrived, everybody knew her, and to me as a young man, she reminded me of the Queen of England. She had her peculiarities, such as asking the waiter to bring her tea bag with her to the restaurant and ask them for a cup of hot water so she could make her tea the way she liked it. She also loved fish and chips. She would put the napkin on her neck and drape it carefully and never dropped any food on her. To this day I can remember her always ordering Piccalilli relish. She would put in on most things that she ate. Piccalilli relish is a relish made from a mixture of chopped and pickled vegetables, spices, and vinegar. It's often made with a base of green tomatoes, onions, and peppers, along with other vegetables like cauliflower, cucumbers, and carrots. Spices like mustard powder, turmeric, and ginger are also commonly used.

My nana also loved fish chowder and would delight in making it for any of her seven grandchildren that would come visit. She also liked to add two spoons of wheat germ to her cereal and in her milk, tea and all her baking projects.

My grandmother never talked about her past growing up or marriage to my grandfather, which was difficult. The most difficult part of her life I am sure was when my father died on February 19th 1968 and my uncle (her other son) died one week later.

My grandmother maintained her dignity, strength, loyalty and compassion and love for me and all the grandchildren until the day she died. I learned from her to maintain a positive attitude when having good times and bad, and always move forward in life and never look back.

I took some of her advice which helped me deal with the loss of my son Max at the age of 20 on February 18th 2004 from complications related to leukemia.

Nana, I think of you often, and I know you're proud of me in the decisions I have made in life. I love you and be well, wherever you are.

Esther (1955- death)

My grandmother Esther, who was my mother's mom, was called Bubbie. She was very loved and respected by all members of our very large family. She sometimes reminded me of the women in the well-known picture of Ma and Pa Kettle or Granny in the well-known television series *The Beverly Hillbillies*.

"Bubbie" and "Zayde" are Yiddish terms for grandmother and grandfather, respectively. These terms are often used in Jewish families, particularly those with Eastern European roots, as informal ways to address or refer to grandparents.

Bubbie could be stern at times but also had a heart of gold. Funny thing, her maiden name was Hassenfeld, and her married name was Gold, just like Barbara's maiden name of Gold. Bubbie commanded respect, and she and my Zayde had a very long and happy marriage together.

Bubbie always knew if I did anything good or bad. She never had to tell me. I could see it in her face. She always told me that I could be and do anything that I put my mind to doing if I would apply myself. Whenever she asked or told me to do something, I never questioned her. I did it out of respect and love for her. Bubbie came from a time back in the 1950's thru the 1980's when respect was given when it was earned. My Bubbie would be very upset how the world is today, and she is surely missed.

Bubbie, I know you're proud of me, and I always love you. Rest in Peace.

Shirley (1955-death)

My mother, Shirley Gold Dwares, passed away at the age of 77 on March 17, 2008. My mother lived a complicated life. She graduated from the former Bryant and Stratton, now known as Bryant University. She worked for her father, my grandfather, who owned a small novelty company. She also owned a few businesses, which included a nursing uniform company. My dad died at the age of 40 on Feb 18, 1968, leaving my mother a widow with five young children, the oldest 13 years old and the youngest 6 years old. My mother lived like a queen but on a princess's income stream. She loved wearing leopard print clothing, and you always knew when (Shirley) was in the room. My mother told me many times that she would do whatever was necessary to take care of her children, no matter what. I learned from my mom to do whatever is needed to be done to protect my family, without ever backing down. She could, with her style, sometimes pit family members against one another, causing many family feuds. She had a good heart, but sometimes it could be misdirected. Mom, I love you and miss you, and if you're in heaven, which I believe that you are, and get a chance, please tell Max that we miss him and will see him soon, although not too soon.

Barbara (1979- ongoing)

There is so much to talk about the love of my life, and I could talk for hours about her. Many of you know that I like to talk, but for the story I'm telling now, I could leave it as only a few short phrases.

Love of my life

Special

Without her I'd be nothing

I could go on and on, but I only say a few things that are extremely important to me.

I probably said a lot of these in my other books that I have written, but here goes.

We met on March 11, 1979.

We got married on June 29, 1980.

Max was born on Nov 04, 1983.

We bought our first house in Oct. 1985.

Jake was born in July 31, 1990.

Max passed away on Feb 18, 2004, at the age of 20.

We bought our current house on Oct 10, 2017.

Life has had its ups and downs but mostly ups.

Tell the truth and try not to embellish too much.

And my favorite few words are these:

Change your clothes.

I have never seen those pants before.

I will hide those clothes if you don't wear something else.

Why don't you wear your new sandals?

Slow down when you eat, talk, and drive.

And most importantly, every time she leaves the house, she calls me a few minutes later to say, "I Love You."

So, all I can say about Barbara is "NEED I say anything more?"

Would You Believe the Following Stories?

Max and Sleep Study and Duffel bag (1989)

Our late son Max lived life, but only for 20 short years. Max was in a very bad car accident when he was quite young but never complained. Instead, he decided to live life fast and furious as if he knew his time on this planet would be short-lived.

Max was always a tough sleeper. When he was about six years old, he would get up at all hours, and even when he was a baby, he would get up and down. We tried to figure out why he constantly woke up. No one in the house could get any sleep, so our PCP recommended we contact the local behavioral hospital to arrange for a consultation. A few weeks later, a sleep study expert came to our home and, after asking us what seemed like 50 or so questions, set up a camera in his bedroom to record all his actions and movement overnight. Within a few days, they told us in writing that we were causing Max's restlessness and his constant waking up at all hours of the night.

The reason, they explained, was that when we would go into his room every time that he cried or check on him when he was finally sleeping, we were upsetting his sleep patterns. We immediately stopped checking on him every time he cried and instead purchased a few baby monitors, one in his room, one in ours, and another on our first floor. We could go in his room to check on him if his crying fits lasted more than a few minutes. Eventually, the crying stopped, and we all began to have pleasant nights to sleep, at least most of the time.

By the time that our youngest son Jake was born in 1990, Max was a pretty good sleeper.

A few years later, in 1992, we were contacted by a research lab to see if Max would want to participate in an in-house sleep study at the Bradley Sleep Research Lab in Riverside Rhode Island. The E.P. Bradley Hospital Sleep Research Lab is an internationally recognized center for research and sleep and development.

Max was to be paid $500 to live at the Sleep Lab for four days and nights and could drop out of the study if he decided to and come home.

As his parents, we were able to visit with Max almost at any time, except when he was sleeping. Max, who was getting paid, decided to complete the program.

On the last day of the program, there was a small graduation ceremony where all the participants would get a diploma, the $500 check, along with a copy of the complete study that would benefit Max's and our family's sleeping patterns for years to come. As parents, we were given a tour of the sleep lab and went into Max's room to pack up all his belongings. We were told to bring a small suitcase and duffel bag to stuff all his belongings in. Well, my mind thought of a few small pranks that I could pull at the last minute. While I finished packing, I asked Barbara to go and chat with the sleep study director and ask about other sleep study programs for youngsters and adults. It was only a ruse to get her out of the room. I explained to Max we could prank Mom, but that he needed to get in the duffel bag, and I would almost zipper it shut. I told him I would carry him out to the conference room, and when I put the duffel bag down, he would count to five and begin to move back and forth. He agreed to do the prank, as I convinced him it would be momentous, and he would be talked about for years to come. Since his sense of humor was most like mine, he readily agreed. A few minutes later, I carried the duffel bag with Max inside and walked into the conference room. Barbara asked me where Max was, and I told her he was in the bathroom. A minute later, I put the duffel bag down on the floor, and five or so seconds later, it mysteriously began to move. People were shocked, and some apparently were frightened and thought that the bag was possessed. I bent over and unzipped the bag, and Max's head popped out. When I told Max to get out, the sleep lab

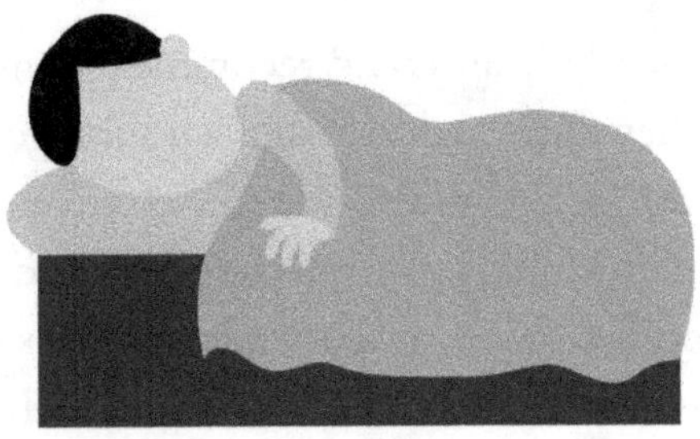

director said that I was wrong for the incident, and he said that I should apologize. I thought about it for a minute or so and then looked the director in the face, who looked like a cross between Albert Einstein and Count Dracula, and I calmly said, "Nah," and off we went. When Max asked me why I didn't apologize, I told him that there are serious times in life (like the sleep study) and other times for a small amount of humor after his four-day sleep study, and I was proud of him, and a good laugh or two was appreciated.

On the way home, if I recall, we stopped for ice cream sundaes, and I was hoping that Max would treat since he just got paid $500, but I got left holding the "bag," or should I say the check...

Shot at close range (1989)

In 1989, I was in Syracuse, NY, with a coworker from the Naval Facilities Engineering Command located in Newport, Rhode Island. We were visiting the General Electric plant that made engine parts for US military airplanes. While checking in to the hotel we were staying at, I was putting my luggage away and turned towards the sunken living room. I tripped down the stairs and ended up with a small scratch on my chest near my throat. It bled a small amount, but I didn't feel that I needed a band-aid. Little did I know that the next day, that small scratch would lead to a night of good food and what appeared at the time to resemble a Mafia-ordered hit on a civilian (meaning an attempted murder on me).

I asked at the hotel if they could recommend a nice Italian restaurant nearby, and they suggested a small place with good food that was also a favorite of the local mafioso. When we arrived, we met a few of the other government employees from the office, and we also saw a few older men with young women, or "goomah," which is Italian-American slang for a mistress. This word is often associated with organized crime. I also saw a few guys standing near the front door who were tall, very muscular, and scary-looking, with what appeared to be no necks; they looked like tree trunks (mob hitmen, perhaps).

Even though I have had a fascination with the Mafia, then and now, I decided to mind my own business and focus on dinner. We ordered our meals and a few drinks and chatted about our visit and what we planned on doing the next few days. Dinner and conversation were going well when I suddenly felt my chest itching, so I began to scratch ever so lightly. Within a minute or so, I felt my chest get a little damp when the guy sitting across from me suddenly stood up and said that I had been shot. There was some panic at our table, and the next thing I knew, two guys from the table in back of me got up with guns drawn and grabbed me and put me under the table. One of them yelled to an employee that they were the FBI and to call 911 to send for backup and an ambulance.

What seemed like an eternity, although only a few minutes, the ambulance arrived with the police and the FBI, and they told everyone to remain at their tables until they were cleared by law enforcement to leave the restaurant. The ambulance attendants came up to me and began to search all over my body for an entrance and exit wound. They also asked if I was in pain and then cut my shirt open. When they couldn't find any wounds, they seemed perplexed. They began to search all over my body and finally saw a small scratch on my chest where I was scratching a few minutes ago. They realized that my scratching my small chest scratches had opened up an area and the blood began to ooze out and soak my shirt red. They smiled a little and told the two

FBI agents that I was ok and the incident was over. After the FBI took statements from everyone, including me, they left the restaurant.

Since I was with other people eating dinner that night, I calmly went into the restroom with a ripped shirt and a soaked red t-shirt. I took them both off and rinsed them in the sink, and using paper towels, I attempted to slightly dry them out. I put on my sport jacket as if nothing had happened and went back to the table to attempt to enjoy my dinner.

The rest of the night at dinner was very funny as my table guests constantly made jokes about shootings, stabbings, Count Dracula, etc. Even though I was a little embarrassed, I know it's all in good humor. When the waiter came over and asked me if I wanted dessert, and I said yes, he said the specialty was blood pudding, and I said, "Very funny." I did ask him, however, why there were FBI agents eating dinner in a mafia restaurant hangout. He explained that even FBI agents love good Italian food, as we did as well.

Jake and Stereo out the window (2005)

In the summer of 2005, the year after Max passed away, Jake was around 15 years old. Barbara and I were having a Fourth of July cookout with friends in our backyard. Jake had quite a few friends over, and they were upstairs in his room enjoying Chinese food that we ordered. They were playing music, and as time went on, the music got louder and louder. I yelled up to Jake and told him to lower the volume, to which he replied, "Okay." No sooner had he lowered the volume than it once again got louder. We heard his gang laughing, yelling, and then screaming. At this time, I went inside, went upstairs, and pounded on the locked door. I banged repeatedly, to which there was no answer at first. Well, since this was Barbara and my home, I kicked at the door like a raving lunatic until he opened it. He was laughing out loud in my face and asked me what the big deal was, that they were blasting the music. I told him that the big deal was this was our house and that we had rules and we expected them to be followed, and to show some respect. Since this was already the second time I politely and diplomatically asked that the music be toned down, I told him if I needed to come upstairs again, he and all his friends would have to suffer the consequences and my wrath.

Would you believe that by the time I got back downstairs, the music was blasting loud and unbearably deafening? I was fuming, and I could almost sense steam billowing out the top of my skull. I knew then that I had to take some sort of action to address the total lack of respect that Jake and his friends had showed me. I thought of a few things off the top of my mind. I could have yelled and screamed at Jake and his friends, but they would have just laughed in my face. I could have sent Jake's friends home, or I could have made Jake and his friends come downstairs and apologize, but that would have been a wasteful and meaningless action, since I couldn't make them actually apologize. So, I did what any rational human being and loving father and parent would do.

What, you might ask, was that? I calmly and gently walked back upstairs and gingerly tapped on the door, to which the reply was, "What's up, dadio?" I replied, "Please unlock and open the door because I have something to say." When I entered the room and stared at them with a face devoid of any emotion other than fury, I could see fear in their faces, as they knew they had crossed the line, and they also could see in my eyes that I was beyond reproach and nothing that they could say or do would resolve the issue at hand.

I calmly walked over to the stereo and unplugged it from the wall outlet. It was fairly heavy, so I put it down below the window. I opened the window as wide as possible and looked at Jake and his friends. Their mouths were wide open, and their eyes opened as well in disbelief.

Jake didn't say a word because he knew I was pissed off at him. I looked down towards the driveway, and by luck, the cars were far enough away from below the window. With a little huffing and puffing, I lifted up the stereo, and with a sense of calm and pleasure, out went the stereo. It smashed into a few large pieces. Do you think that I was done? Of course not. I lifted each of the two rather large speakers, and one at a time, I went towards the window, and out they went. The crash and loud bangs of them hitting the stereo and the cement driveway below was very satisfying indeed. I turned around, and without saying anything, I calmly walked towards the bedroom door and walked down the stairs. I went into the backyard, and Barbara asked me what the loud noises were. When I told her what I had done, she was extremely upset with me, and I knew then, after my friends left our cookout later on that day, she would have a discussion with me. I would not back down and would say I made the decision, and that's that. Later that day, Barbara did indeed have a rather lengthy discussion with me. She told me I could and should have handled the situation at hand by some other means. When I asked her what that would be, she replied I should have sent Jake's friends home and grounded Jake for a month or so. She then asked me why I didn't think of any other method to address the situation, to which I replied, "Barbara, I did think of throwing Jake and his friends out the second story window," to which she said, "Why would I ever think of doing something so dumb and outrageous?" I replied somewhat jokingly, "I didn't do that simply because of all the paperwork and insurance claims I would have been responsible for, not to mention the rather long prison sentence I would have to endure."

Do you think we heard loud music the rest of the afternoon? Of course not. The sounds of the birds chirping and the grill sizzling was all the music I needed to hear. Oh, what sweet sounds, pun intended.

Jake- from sneaky drinker to superior and excellent bar tender and Banana whisky in basement (2006)

Many years ago, in 2006, we were living in our first house on Packard Street in Cranston, RI. We had just renovated our basement, with one half being a laundry room and the other area my workbench. The other side we turned into a playroom and spare bedroom. We also had the water meter and gas meter boxed in to keep them out of sight.

Over the years, our two sons, Max and Jake, both hung out in the finished playroom, and Max even lived downstairs there for a year or two.

A few years after Max passed away, the water company contacted me to inform us that the water meter had to be replaced.

The technician came over, and I showed him where the water meter was located. I went upstairs to take care of a few things, and within a minute or two, he called me to come downstairs to show me something. I went down, and he asked me if we had any alcoholics living in the house. I explained that I abstained from alcohol and that Barbara would occasionally have a light beer when we went out to dinner with friends. The tech told me that he found a treasure trove of booze hidden below the water meter. I looked inside the enclosure and found approximately 25 empty beer cans and bottles, as well as some ½ empty and open whiskey bottles, including banana whiskey, vodka, and rum, among others.

Since I knew that I didn't drink and that Barbara only consumed a light beer every once in a while, there had to be only two possible suspects fitting this crime. It could have been either Max, but he had passed away a few years ago, so that left only Jake to interrogate.

We sat Jake down, who by then was 16 years old and too young to buy liquor.

Jake told me that he found the bottles left by Max, and he and his friends would have drinking parties in the basement and hide everything so we obviously wouldn't find them. One of the bottles that wasn't opened was banana whisky.

For many years after, Barbara would look for the same bottle of banana whisky to toast Max and our family.

As for Jake, we never grounded him for drinking booze in our house because we knew he could drink and smoke, and we would never find out. Instead, we took it as a learning experience for Jake and told him moderation in drinking would be appropriate.

Many years later, as I am writing this book, Jake is happily married and works full time in the field of cyber security. He also works part time as a bartender at a local establishment where he serves drinks to hopefully mature patrons.

I guess you could say that Jake got his early bartending training way back in 2006 when he allegedly got his training from bottles of booze that were hidden behind a water heater.

Navy SEALs Overboard (2009)

In 2009, I was the senior contracting officer for the United States Naval War College, located in Newport, Rhode Island. I was responsible for negotiating and awarding multi-million-dollar contracts for the Navy. Among my other duties, I would visit military bases all over the United States and see the development of helicopters, ships, and weapon systems. Occasionally, I would be allowed to participate in some of the testing trials for these ships and weapon systems.

On one such occasion, I was invited to be a member of the Navy SEALs program that was developing top-secret vessels and weapon systems.

The Navy SEALs, officially known as United States Navy Sea, Air, and Land Teams, are the U.S. Navy's primary special operations force. They are highly trained and specialize in direct action, special reconnaissance, and unconventional warfare.

I was told to show up to one of the boat docks at the Navy base in Newport. When I arrived, there was a boat with a driver, two engineers, a few Navy SEALs, and myself, for a total of six people. The boat that I was on was experimental and had four 500-horsepower engines; it could reach a maximum speed of 60-70 mph, if need be. It sounds like a James Bond story, but it actually was way ahead of its time, and experimentation of these crafts received full and unlimited funding by the US Department of Defense (DOD). This boat was being built to be used to rescue hostages from beachheads worldwide.

It meant that, in the event of Americans being held hostage, these boats could be launched from a giant aircraft carrier or be remote-controlled. The back of the boat had space for four jet skis that could be jettisoned on the beachhead. When the hostages were being rescued, they could be driven back to the boat, and the people could be taken to safety.

Most times, the Navy SEALs were very professional but could also be crazy and do things you never expect. On one such occasion, we were speeding towards Block Island, which is located in the Atlantic Ocean, approximately 12 miles off the southern coast of Rhode Island and 21 miles east of Montauk Point on Long Island. It's part of the Outer Lands archipelago and is actually in the town of New Shoreham, in Rhode Island. The island is known for its natural beauty, including dramatic bluffs, rolling hills, and pristine beaches.

While speeding around 70 miles an hour, I was sitting at the front of the boat with the driver; the two engineers were in the middle, and the two Navy SEALs were sitting on the very back of the boat.

As I was holding on for dear life as the boat banged against the waves, I was scared shitless. After a few minutes, I turned around and the Navy SEALs were gone. I motioned to the driver to turn around immediately and to call the Coast Guard with a distress signal, reporting two people overboard. He did, and also called the US Coast Guard, who immediately sent a helicopter to join in the search. After searching for an hour with no results, we headed back to the base, where I had to inform the base commander, who ordered me to fill out a report to be given to him the next morning at 0700 hours. A little after 7:30 the next morning, I was sitting in my office, still very upset from the day before. All of a sudden, I heard a knock on my door, and who do you think it was? It was the two Navy SEALs, who began to laugh their asses off. They told me that they were testing a cigar-sized oxygen canister and they went overboard on purpose. They had prearranged for the Coast Guard to fly over and pick them up at the exact coordinates that they sent them, and they said they were just doing the job that they were trained for. They told me that they were not sorry at all that they scared the shit out of me, and they laughed out loud. I realized then, and still do today many years later, that many things happen in life that are unexplainable, and there's no rhyme or reason to them.

The moral of this (true) story is I always knew the Navy SEALs and the Delta Force members were somewhat crazy, but they do the dirty work for the United States of America, and they didn't give a damn

what I, you, or anyone else thinks. Their only goal is to complete the mission at hand, no more and no less.

I learned that day that the core moral principles of Navy SEALs revolve around loyalty, integrity, leadership, and courage. These values, embodied in the SEAL ethos, guide their actions both on and off the battlefield. They are committed to their country and team, unwavering in their commitment to uphold the highest standards of conduct. The SEALs use many different expressions that reflect their unique mindset. Some of the most common are "Hoya", "the only easy day was yesterday," and "it pays to be a winner". God Bless America and God bless our troops.

CVS in Sanford, Maine - No bathroom (2025).

While visiting Ogunquit, Maine, in March 2025, Barbara and I took a short road trip to Sanford, Maine, about 19 miles away, further north. The drive took us through some long and winding roads, and we went through some rural areas with older homes and businesses. By the time we arrived, I needed to take a potty break. We found a local CVS, and I got out of the car right away and ran into the store as quick as O.J. Simpson was running through the airport in the American Tourister luggage commercial of many years ago.

I was holding my breath and sweating, looking for the bathroom, and asked a store employee where it was located.

I was informed that the bathroom was unavailable for use since it was being used as a storage room for excessive goods that had no space to display.

I was told that there was a Cumberland Farms about ½ a mile away. I told the clerk that I was serious about using the bathroom, but he insisted that there wasn't one available.

I wasn't happy about that, but like Superman, aka Clark Kent, I flew out of the store, got in the front seat, and peeled rubber down the road. Being in Maine, I should have realized that things here were a lot slower than living in the big city of Cranston, RI. The only thing here that was quick was probably just peeling potatoes. I will leave you with a favorite Maine slang word, "Ayuh," which means "yes" or "sure." That's all I can say about Maine.

Wrong Place Wrong Time

Hostess Snoballs in Supermarket (1972)

In 1972, I was 17 years old and didn't have a care in the world. Life was good. My father had died in 1968, and I was finally coming out of my funk, now known most likely as a depression. I had a car, a girlfriend or two, a part-time job, and some spending cash in my pocket. I was a skinny kid, weighing in at a respectable weight of 140 pounds, with an afro and a heck of a lot of hair. Did I mention I was also a good-looking dude?

One day, I decided to go shopping for some groceries for my mom and went to the supermarket on North Main Street in Providence that used to be Star Market. It is now a Whole Foods Market.

I didn't eat a lot of junk food back then, but I sure did love eating Hostess Snoballs.

True Snoball eaters know that Hostess Snoball cakes are the all-around champs of snacking. With their signature pink coconut topping, fluffy marshmallow coating, soft chocolate cake, and sweet, creamy center, they are delicious.

Today, they come in many different colors, I assume to match the holidays, like green for Easter and orange for Halloween, for example. On the day in question, I was doing my shopping when I came by the aisle of snacks, and immediately my eyes were fixated on the pink snoball cakes that I loved to devour. I opened a package while walking through the aisles, and I ate the two snoballs, which had a heavenly taste. I dropped the wrapper in the carriage and fully intended to pay for them on the way out of the store. By the time I got to the checkout aisle, 15 or 20 minutes had gone by, and I put my groceries up on the small conveyor belt so the clerk could charge me for them. I can't recall how much the groceries cost back then, but I am sure it was much cheaper than today in 2025. I paid my bill and waited for the cashier to bag them for me. I whistled, turned, and headed towards the front door when all of a sudden I saw a policeman walk towards me from outside. He asked me how I was doing, and I said, "Fine, and you sir," and I was about to go my merry way. The policeman asked me if I forgot anything, and I said I didn't think so, and then he pointed to the empty package of snoballs on the bottom of my carriage. He asked me if I intended to pay for them, and I said, "I'm so sorry, I forgot about them." He did mention to me that if I stepped two more feet outside the door, he would have to arrest me for shoplifting, or I could go back in the store and pay for the item that I ate, namely the snoballs. Of course, by then, everyone in the store saw and heard what I had done, and the policeman stood right next to me when I got back in line and waited with everybody else to pay my bill. I was very embarrassed and vowed to never let that happen again.

Back in 1972, the two-pack of snoballs probably cost about 30 cents, while today, in 2025, they probably cost $2.50 a pack.

Once I was done paying, the policeman was waiting at the front of the store and made me turn around one more time so everyone shopping could see that I was a potential shoplifter.

I learned a valuable lesson that day: to never eat anything while walking around the store, and if I do, make sure I keep the empty package on the top of everything so I would not forget to pay.

Hindsight: Do I think the policeman would have arrested me for stealing $0.30 worth of dessert? The answer is most likely yes because back then, respect and doing the right thing was more important than it seems to be today.

Play Ball, or should I say (Snoball)?

Tweet Balzano's Family Restaurant (1973)

In 1973, I was a student at Roger Williams University, located in Bristol, RI, and working on my associate's degree in Psychology. Life was good. On one occasion, a few of my friends and I went to Tweet Balzano's restaurant in Bristol, which specialized in pasta, seafood, and Italian-style dishes. My friends ordered some type of pasta dishes with clams. Although I no longer eat seafood, I used to always order steamers. Steamed clams are a seafood dish of clams cooked in a covered pot with a splash of liquid, like wine, water, or chicken stock. The clams release their own liquid as they cook and are considered ready when their shells open, which can take 5-10 minutes. The dish is often served with crusty bread and a glass of wine. I loved them and ate them as often as possible. On one of my many visits to the restaurant, I placed my order. The steamers came out piping hot, just how I liked them. I ate a half dozen or so until I heard a crunch. I spit out a small stone, but luckily, I didn't break any teeth. I called the waiter over and explained the situation. He said that the kitchen staff does their best to clean the steamers, but occasionally they may have a rock in them. He immediately offered to bring me another dish, which he did. The second order was delicious. When we were done eating, the waiter came over and gave each of us our individual checks. Steamers back then were about $5-6 dollars a dish, so I was surprised to see two orders charged on my check. I told the waiter, but he refused to delete the second order of steamers that he charged on my check. I said I wasn't going to pay, and he said he'd call the police if I refused.

Of course, I refused. A short time later, a Bristol policeman arrived, came to my table, and asked me what the problem was. I explained the situation, and he said that I was responsible to pay the entire bill. He told me that if I didn't pay, he would place me under arrest and that I had two minutes to decide. I noticed his name on his badge, and would you believe it? It was Balzano's. Well, of course, I asked if he was any relation to the owners of the restaurant, to which he replied, "They are my aunt and uncle." After hearing that, I decided that it would be best if I paid the bill. I told him that I felt that the situation should have been resolved by the manager, but I knew that would be futile. I told the policeman that I would never go back to the restaurant again, to which he replied, "I hope to never see you again." My reply to him was, "The feelings are mutual." Do you think I ever saw him again? Of course, I did, when he arrested me a few years later when I accidentally cut off a firetruck in Bristol, RI, and he was the police officer at the scene of the incident.

Footnote: I had told myself that I would never again go to Tweet Balzano's restaurant in Bristol ever again, but to be quite honest, my wife and I, along with my son Jake and his wife and daughter, went to dinner there in 2014, shortly before it went out of business. Even though the "steamer incident" happened in 1973, more than 41 years earlier, I still had an uneasy feeling as we dined there that night.

Kevin arrested cutting off firetruck (1975)

In 1975, I was arrested for mistakenly cutting off a fire truck in Bristol, Rhode Island, where I was a student at Roger Williams University. The policeman's name was Balzano, a well-known name in Bristol. Would you believe he was the same policeman who almost arrested me a few years before? (See my story entitled "Tweet Balzano's"). I was driving my 1974 Triumph Spitfire convertible through town, and I was probably driving too fast. I was on Hope Street and had my radio blasting, and then it happened. Out of nowhere came a fire truck, and at the very last minute, I inadvertently cut in front of him, and he missed smashing into me by a mere 20-30 feet.

Many years later, I still can remember the street called Hope Street. This street is intersected by Burton Street, Wood Street, Franklin Street, Church Street, and Noyes Avenue.

As the truck blared its horn, I just continued on my merry way and didn't think much about it, since I knew I didn't cut him off on purpose and felt I did nothing wrong except maybe having my music on too loud, which hampered my ability to hear his horn blaring.

I continued on Hope Street, and within two to three minutes, a car got behind me and began to flash its lights on and off. He then got fairly close to my back bumper and kept beeping his horn. I must admit I gave him the one-finger salute, and I did tap the brakes a few times to attempt to have him back off. Next, I sped up as fast as I could. Within a minute or two, three police cars were in front of me with the officers leaned over the hoods of their cars with guns drawn and pointed at me. I, of course, stopped instantly, and then they yelled for me to get out of the car ever so slowly and told me to put my hands behind my back and walk back toward them. The next thing I knew, I was in handcuffs, and they slammed me headfirst into the hood of my car. One of the police officers was screaming at me, and another one asked if I had any weapons or drugs on me, and of course, I said no. One of them said he wanted my permission to open my trunk, to which I allowed him to do.

Another officer read me the Miranda rights, which give protections for individuals during police questioning after they have been taken into custody.

I realized then that I was in trouble, so I was as cooperative as possible. I was put in the back of a patrol car and kept my mouth shut. I was taken to the police station and brought into a holding cell. My shoelaces and belt were taken off; they told me that they were afraid I could commit suicide. While I was being processed, they asked me if I had any questions. I said I wanted to make a phone call. They asked whom I wanted to call, and I said my uncle. They said okay and to make it quick. I called my uncle, who was a dentist and was very politically connected and had some friends who were judges. My uncle told me not to say anything to anybody and that his friend the judge would be calling the police chief shortly. In the holding cell, the policeman on duty read the charges against me. If I recall, it was evading arrest, cutting off a fire truck in the middle of a fire, threatening a police officer, speeding, threatening language, speeding down a side street, and many other charges too numerous to remember. After they went over the charges, I was told that I would be released on my own personal recognizance and that I would have a court date in the future. I didn't realize that a judge had called the police chief (thanks to my uncle) to clear up the event on my behalf, of course. Five or so minutes later, the police chief himself came down to my holding cell, opened the door, and told me I was free to go. He then said I must have friends in high places. I asked for my keys back from my car, but my car was still a few miles away, and the police refused to take me to it. No problem, since it was a nice day, so I walked. Sure enough, two or three weeks later, I had a court date, and an attorney showed up for me. When I got in front of the judge, he said there was an error in the police report, which allowed them to drop all the charges against me. What he meant to say was that a high-ranking politician put the fix in to drop all the charges against me.

I did apologize publicly in court to all the police and all the court officials, and I admitted that I was wrong and was sorry.

Since Bristol, Rhode Island, was a small town and everybody knew one another, I was given advice from the judge, who told me the police would always be looking for me anytime they could give me a ticket or harass me. Lucky for me, this was towards the end of my sophomore year of college, and I transferred out of Roger Williams University that year. I have never gotten into any more trouble in Bristol ever again.

Dave's Bar and Grill (1998)

In 1998, my wife and I were friends with a Jewish couple who were fairly religious but would occasionally go out to dinner at a restaurant, though they would only eat kosher food and order fish or salads.

The husband of the couple was an emergency room doctor and would usually come home late from work due to never knowing when the last patient would be taken care of.

On one such occasion, we decided to make plans and meet them at a local restaurant in Warwick, RI, near the airport, for dinner. Barbara and I arrived at the restaurant early, and a few minutes later, the wife of our friends arrived. We chatted for a while about our children and our occupations, and the time seemed to fly by. I was beginning to get hungry, and by then, a half hour had gone by, and the doctor still hadn't arrived. I said that we should order dinner and not wait any longer for the doctor to arrive. The three of us, Barbara, my friend, and I, ordered dinner. A few minutes after their dinner was served, my friend's husband showed up.

The wife and husband started arguing with one another and blamed each other for something that we didn't quite understand. Finally, the doctor ordered his food, which arrived approximately 15 minutes later. The couple began to argue again, and then, out of nowhere, the wife took a huge handful of steak fries from her plate and threw them in her husband's face.

They both got up and screamed at one another as I tried to calm them down, but to no avail. The manager came over and asked us all to leave the restaurant and told us we were never welcome to come there again. We all got up and left the restaurant and, since 1998, have never returned. This wasn't the first or the last time that we were ever banned from a restaurant, but you can confidently be made aware that it never happened because of anything that Barbara or I did or participated in. Perhaps those stories will be told at a later date and time.

Woman at Whole Foods / Florida Hurricane (2022)

In 2022, Florida suffered another blow from a major hurricane, this time named Ian. The town of Fort Myers Beach took a catastrophic direct hit from Hurricane Ian on Wednesday, Sept. 28, 2022. Ian was a category 4-plus hurricane with winds between 130 - 156 miles per hour. Most of Fort Myers and the West Coast was destroyed. A week or so after the Hurricane, I happened to be in Whole Foods in Garden City looking for chicken hot dogs for Maya, my granddaughter, who is precious, as she frequently tells me. While shopping, a woman approximately 50-plus happened to be looking in the same cooler cases as I was. I excused myself as she tried to go in the case that I was in. I commented that she had a very nice tan, to which she replied, "It doesn't fucking matter since my home was totally destroyed in the Florida Hurricane." She then began to cry, so I spent some time chatting with her. The woman, whose name was Laila, looked like she was an actress in a Hollywood film. She was manicured, well-tanned, beautiful, sexy, and highly intelligent. I thought about the movie called "10," starring Bo Derek from many years ago, about a stunning beauty released in the late 1970s.

She asked me if I had time since she had a story to tell. I said of course because I love telling stories myself. She explained that in mid-August 2022, she and her husband both retired from corporate executive positions and had sold their house in Western Cranston, RI, for over $600,000 and used it to purchase a home in Fort Myers, Florida. She said that her and her husband's dream had been to retire in their mid- to late-'50s and move to Fort Myers, where they had been many times before with their children. While looking for a home that they planned to pay cash for, they settled on one very close to the beach in Fort Myers. Since they did not plan on having a mortgage, and the house would come first with hurricane windows and doors, they decided not

to pay for flood insurance as it was not required in this location. She said that while Florida state law didn't mandate flood insurance for all homeowners, it was recommended, especially given the state's coastal nature and potential for flooding. But as she mentioned, they weren't taking a mortgage, so they decided to save the $3,000 to $4,000 a year and not purchase flood insurance. She said that the realtor did not mention anything about her own homeowner's insurance not covering floods, so she assumed it would be covered in the event of a catastrophe.

After the real estate transaction closed on her new house in Florida, she came back to Rhode Island for a few weeks to settle all the outstanding issues with bills, doctors, insurance, etc. They planned on returning to Florida around the 30th of September or, at the latest, during October 2022.

While staying with family in Rhode Island, they got a call on September 28, 2022, that a friend living near Fort Myers told her that her house and many nearby were missing, as they were destroyed during the hurricane and washed out to sea. The first thing she did was call her homeowners insurance company, who told her floods were not covered. She was devastated and advised to call FEMA (Federal Emergency Management Agency), which said they could provide assistance for flood damage, both through its disaster assistance programs and through the National Flood Insurance Program (NFIP). However, FEMA's assistance is not meant to replace flood insurance, and it's important to understand the different types of assistance available. The maximum amount of assistance FEMA offered at that time was $42,500. As Laila continued with her story, she became more and more agitated and sad. She told me she and her husband were lucky that they had some family in Cranston where they could stay for a while until they tried to figure out where they would live and how they could afford it. She told me, when she was about to finish shopping, that they rolled the dice and this time they lost, and their loss was over $600,000. I gently hugged her and wished her luck in all that she needed to do to figure out the next steps in her life. I left the store thinking how lucky Barbara and I were. We decided we would never move to Florida or anywhere else that had hurricanes and bad storms.

Sanford, Maine, and Deliverance (2025)

While visiting Ogunquit, Maine, on March 25, 2025, Barbara and I decided to take a day trip to Sanford, Maine, approximately 30-40 minutes further north. We were told that the area had a nice small downtown area with many shops and restaurants to enjoy lunch. We took the back roads and enjoyed some of the scenery but noticed a lot of rundown and dilapidated properties along the way. At one point, I mentioned that the area reminded me of parts of the movie "Deliverance." The movie was about four friends who leave their jobs and decide to go camping in rural Georgia and do some rafting and get away from society. They, however, didn't realize that they were going into the backwoods where the locals did not like outsiders and tried to kill them.

The first place we stopped was a gas station since I needed to use the bathroom. I knew right away that there may be an issue since the bathroom door was locked. I asked the clerk and he handed me a key that was on the end of a huge metal stick about three feet long.

After I was done in the bathroom, I returned the key and asked why it was at the end of the metal stick. The clerk said, "Where you from, boy?" I said, "Rhode Island," and he said where was that, but I realized he was not joking.

He said people who weren't from Maine should stay the hell out since he felt big box stores like Lowe's and Walmart were ruining Maine. I told him that doesn't make any sense, to which he said then get out of his store and don't let the door hit me in the ass. I thanked him for his hospitality, to which he smiled, and I then noticed he only had a few teeth in his mouth, probably used to open the can of cat food or tuna fish that he probably was going to eat for lunch that day. As we began to drive away, I told Barbara of my experience, and she said that we should look for a new store that was called "Ollie's" that was supposed to be nearby. We had been to one in Florida a few years back. That's what I began to think we were in that area, like in the movie *Deliverance*, or for you horror aficionado's, *The Texas Chainsaw Massacre*. As we arrived at the parking lot of Ollie's, we saw a big sign, and it said that it would be opening soon. We were disappointed.

We then went to a thrift store nearby and saw three guys there with denim jackets and filthy shoes and boots, and when they all smiled, I noticed that they talked just like actors in the LL Bean television commercials. One of them saw my license plate, "Rhode Island," and said, "What are you city slickers doing in Maine?" When I replied shopping, one of them said okay and let out a large belch and said that we should enjoy our time.

I decided then that it was time to get in the car and go back to civilization as soon as possible. I would have hated to break down on the back roads that had no lights and probably no running water or electricity.

And did I mention I heard a lot of Ayuh. The first word of most

Maine-born babies. Maine's version of y'all or aloha, ayuh is an essential part of the local vocabulary. Uttered once or many times in rapid succession, ayuh means a very strong yes. That's all from Maine "Ayuh."

YOU probably are hoping that I am almost finished with my newest book. Not yet, but soon. What else could you possibly want or need to do? This book is probably the most exciting thing that you have read in many years (LOL).

So as not to put you to sleep after reading my latest and hopefully greatest book (at least in my mind), I have decided to conclude this book with two final items of interest (and a bonus story), and should I say items that interest me and most likely only me:

1. The five books of Moses and Kevin

You've heard of The Five Books of Moses, which are Genesis, Exodus, Leviticus, Numbers, and Deuteronomy. They contain the story of creation.

While I don't profess to be an overly religious person (I actually think I am more of a spiritual type), I think sometimes that mankind should get back to the ideals and laws of the past. Perhaps going back to what is allegedly preached in the ten commandments would do us all well.

NEED I SAY MORE?

And now that you know a little more about the Five Books Of Moses, I will direct your attention to the other set of five books, namely the "Five Books Of Kevin," and they are: *Live to the Max* (this book is about my late son Max, who passed away at the age of 20 on Feb 18, 2004), *A Royal Crowning Achievement*, which is about my extensive dental work during Covid, *Right Place Right Time*, about me being, of course, at the Right Place and the Right Time, *Right Place Right Time Part 2,* a continuation of the prior book, *Right Place Right Time,* and finally the book that you are hopefully reading and enjoying entitled: "Would You Believe?" This book title says it all. Now enough about me and plugging my books, although they are all available in the Cranston RI library system and also on Amazon.com. Note: All proceeds are sent to The Tomorrow Fund at RI Hospital to benefit children and their families dealing with Cancer.

2. And now my final story, which I call my **EULOGY**. Most of the readers may wonder why in his right mind Kevin Dean Dwares would write about himself when they must assume he is still living since he is writing this story. I will leave that up to you to decide. The truth is I am very much alive, and I am writing this story during the month of December 2025. The truth is I have thought about my life for many years and have often wondered what people would honestly say about me after I was planted in the ground.

I will first tell you what the word *eulogy* actually means.

I can summarize in a few short sentences. A eulogy is a speech or writing that lavishes praise, typically about someone who has died. Based upon my own understanding, it should reflect the character, personality, achievements, and values of the person who has passed away. I would like to put in my own two words here, or many more, but since I am writing my own eulogy, I may go on and on, but at least not forever.

Most people, perhaps including myself, would and probably should be asking why in the world Kevin wrote his own eulogy. If I may say so myself, I am in fairly good health. I exercise daily, I eat healthily, although sometimes I do consume a lot of ice cream against the advice of my gastroenterologist and also the advice given to me by my life partner (in my dreams)-no, not Raquel Welch, may she rest in peace-but the advice from my wife of 45-plus years, Barbara Gold Dwares. She always tells me that I don't understand or listen to the word "moderation."

I will let you know up front that some of you may not like my words or tone, but you should consider yourself lucky that I am not mentioning your name, though you know who you are. And most importantly, I am DEAD, so I can say whatever I fucking feel like saying, and if you're upset with me, why not get off your high horse and take a one-way ride up to heaven? I will gladly save you a seat at the table and open the pearly gates in heaven for you as well, if you so desire to join me.

Some of you, and perhaps many of you, won't like the tone of my speech or the words, but I know that many of you wish you had the "gonads" to truly say what's on your mind. Should-heaven forbid-the love of my life, Barbara Gold Dwares, not predecease me, I do apologize to her and my son Jake, his wife Maria, and my one and only and favorite grandchild, Maya, if this eulogy should upset them. Just in case it does, then I promise when we all meet up again up in heaven many years from now, they have my permission to smack me across the face, and I will humbly accept it. And now to get on with the festivities.

My Eulogy (Written by Kevin Dean Dwares and read aloud at my funeral by my Rabbi)

Good afternoon, friends, relatives, and also some of you who were always assholes and are only here today because you felt that you had an obligation to attend my funeral. More likely, you planned on coming over to my home after my funeral in Garden City, Cranston, to feast on some good kosher deli, lox, and bagels. For you few people I never liked or ever respected, I will say it as plain as can be. The world is filled with mostly good and kind people, and there are always a few bad apples. But lucky for me, I have been privileged to know most of you and your kind hearts, and I thank you for your love and friendship over the years, and I say "thank you."

While today may be a somber day for some of you, I am up in Heaven with G-D and the supreme angels, and I don't mean Diana Ross and the Supremes.

How I got to Heaven is the same story that all of us here live through, and eventually fate will get us all.

There is a date that G-D selects for each of us to come home to his grace and kindness.

There is a prayer in the Jewish religion that includes the lines "Some die by fire and some by flood," etc. The prayer in English is called the Unetaneh Tokef. This prayer is recited on Rosh Hashanah and Yom Kippur, the High Holy Days, and is a meditation on death and judgment. The lines in the prayer are part of the prayer's contemplation of how people will die, referencing different ways of death.

With so much uncertainty in the world, there is one thing we can say with 100% certainty: we will all die. Death is a fact of life, but that doesn't make it any less tragic. Nearly 3 million people in the US died in 2024, and approximately 62 million people worldwide died the same year. Believe it or not, almost 109 billion humans have died throughout history according to estimates from the "population reference bureau." Some died of old age after living long lives, while others were killed by cancer, heart disease, respiratory diseases, and even at the hands of fellow human beings. Unetaneh Tokef reminds us of the scary, but very real fact of our mortality and vulnerability.

It's interesting, but whether you be rich or poor, black or white, good or evil, we all fall into the same phase. The only thing certain in life is death and taxes, although a few of us may cheat on our taxes and actually get away with it; no one, to the best of my knowledge, has ever cheated death if G-D had determined that it is their time to depart the earth.

It doesn't really matter as it won't change anything, but we also can Google and see more or less what our individual life expectancy is.

In 2023, the average life expectancy for men in the United States was 75.8 years, while for women, it was 81.1 years. This means that, on average, women live about 5.3 years longer than men in the US.

There are many factors that contribute to the difference between men and women regarding life expectancy, but I would rather talk about me.

You may wonder why I would care about if women live longer than men, or how people die. I don't really care at all, but for the sake of me rambling on, I thought some basic context would be of interest. If not, then feel free to go back to your short cat nap, as the Rabbi hopefully is continuing his praise of me.

I have lived, or so I thought, a relatively healthy and productive life.

I have also had my share of health issues, many good and some bad, that you may not have known about:

I had thyroid cancer detected in 2005 and had my thyroid removed. I take a synthetic pill called levothyroxine to help me live a healthy life.

I had triple hernia surgery around 2015, if I recall.

I have chronic dry eye, which occasionally causes blurry vision.

I have AFIB that was detected in the summer of 2024. In case you care, AFIB is atrial fibrillation, which can cause a chronic elevated heart rate, which makes me a higher risk of a heart attack or stroke. I was prescribed **diltiazem,** which is a calcium channel blocker used to disrupt the movement of calcium in one's system. I was also prescribed Eliquis, which is a blood thinner used to prevent blood clots and strokes, which can kill people, and it does many times annually.

I will briefly tell you a little more about me and how I lived.

Work- I spent most of my career as a loyal federal servant with the U.S. Government. Even though some of you may have thought I may have worked as a double agent for the Cuban or the Russian government, this is totally preposterous. I also never worked for the IRS, KGB, FBI, or the CIA. If you ask me what I did, my response would most likely be, "If I tell you, I would have to kill you." It's up to you to read between the lines. It's also possible that my file may be under lock and key and won't be available for the public to get access to it until 50 years after my demise. Don't bother asking my wife Barbara or my son Jake what I did, since Jake always thought I was a maintenance man, and Barbara never knew what I did. If you think I am bullshitting you, that is ok, but always remember that truth is sometimes simpler than fiction. I leave you with that.

Volunteer- I did a lot of volunteer work over the years, from delivering meals on wheels to mainly homebound elderly, to spending time in soup kitchens and many other similar social service agencies.

Donation- My wife Barbara and I collected many items, such as clothing, shelf-stable food, and toiletries, and brought them to agencies that were in need of them so they could distribute them.

Airport- I volunteer as a greeter at the information center at T.F. Green International Airport.

I volunteered at the Tomorrow Fund at RI Hospital for children with cancer.

I am a member of Touro Fraternal Association, which is a Jewish men's group that emphasizes social and charitable activities.

I am a member of Chabad of West Bay in Warwick, RI, which is a Jewish religious organization committed to strengthening Jewish community and much more.

Since I am now DEAD and someone is reading my eulogy, I may not have a clue how I died, but I hope it was simply a case of old age.

Time doesn't slow down for anyone. The clock ticks until it stops, like what happens when a battery runs out of its usefulness.

I hope to see you all on the other side.

I hope I didn't bore you with too many details about death, but I have come to realize that it's nothing to fear.

To simplify it, I would like my eulogy to say these few things:

We are gathered here today to celebrate the life of Kevin Dean Dwares. He was a good father, father-in-law, grandfather, and brother. He was a wonderful husband and friend to all.

Now get the hell out here and bury me and get on with your life. Life is for the living, so live it.

Live your life each and every day. Don't live by checklists as most people do by having shopping lists, doctor appointments, and everything always being pre-scheduled.

Many of my older friends and confidants like to talk about how old they are, how sick they are, how many prescriptions they take, etc. Talking about death is less important to me since most people (unless you're lucky and you can outrace and cheat death) I believe only die once. It's better to live and love life every day. When people ask (after I died) how he died, I would much rather they reply, "Let me tell you how he lived."

I will conclude this chapter with a famous quote attributed to Rabbi Tzvi Freeman, a Canadian rabbi and author associated with the Chabad-Lubavitch Hasidic movement. (I was given written permission to use it in this story.)

"Life does not tell stories. People do.
Life provides raw materials, raw enough for us to look back and construct at least two versions of our own biography-its past, its present, and its future: one a dungeon, the other a palace."
This is the greatest kindness the Master of Life has given us: He has placed His own pen in our hands that we may enjoy the dignity of life constructed by our own design."
We can't go back into the past. We can't go forward into the future. We can only live in the present, so you better live it the best you can.

Bonus Stories

About a Busy Time from July 2025-November 2025

I know that most of you are finally glad to be at the end of my book, [but] I have a small surprise for you. It ain't done yet. I want to leave you all with a bonus story about a few busy months we had during July and November 2025. While most of you could[n't] care less about this bonus story, some of you may have experienced a similar week and may actually enjoy reading this. Each and every one of us has had stress in our lives, but it's how you deal with it that matters. In all honesty, my life has been great, and the few months I will discuss next were simply part of the journey.

We had planned to have a new small deck built next to our garage and were told that it would only take a week in mid-July 2025, or somewhat longer. Naturally, this wasn't the case. The contractor did a great job, but, through no fault of his, he ran into a few unforeseen issues. One of the items that needed to be addressed was [that] when he ripped off the original trek decking, he found a set of concrete steps. He first thought they could remain in place.

However, this was not to be the case. Since I had a building permit, it required that the cement footings (what holds the deck in place) be higher and necessitated the concrete stairs to be jackhammered away. This was no simple task. Lo and behold, after the steps were removed, it was determined that no cement wall was keeping the stairs in place, so a new wall had to be built in place. This, of course, added additional time and $$$$$ for the project since the building inspector had to come out to our home on three separate times to give approval for the work being done. We also had some extremely hot days with heavy humidity, and on some of these days, the contractor either sent his crew home early, or they simply didn't work that day at all.

During this time, we also had to deal with a bad rain and wind storm on Thursday, July 3, and July 4, 2025, that pelted Rhode Island and the rest of the East Coast.

We lost a large tree in the front yard, and I had to hire a tree removal service to take it down and grind out the stump as well.

Lucky for us, we asked a neighbor about a tree in their yard called a tulip tree. We asked where they got it. They said from the Warwick/ Cranston Land Trust, which provides free trees and installation. We contacted them immediately, and the tree was delivered and planted in early Oct 2025.

We also had no power (electricity) from Thursday night until midafternoon Friday, so the contractor couldn't do any work.

To add insult to injury, we got a flat tire on Friday morning, July 04, 2025. As we were turning into Garden City, I didn't notice that a lot of rocks, some big and some small, had fallen onto the road, and I ran over them. Later that day, I had a new tire put on at a whopping cost of $203.20. I contacted the city since I felt they should be held responsible. They told me that it's a state road and that they have put me in touch with DOT, who, as of me writing this, are reviewing it to determine if they are at fault. I won't hold my breath, or my head may explode.

During this same glorious week, the canopy cover on our backyard glider ripped during the storm, so I had to order a new top. The funny thing is, a box was delivered with the canopy that had nuts and bolts with it. They didn't seem to belong, so I threw the box in the trash. Luckily for me, the trash wasn't picked up until a few days later. Why, you ask, does this matter? It mattered because the contractor was looking for a box with some special hardware, which he said he had delivered to our house. You guessed it. The box was part of our deck project and not the canopy for our outdoor glider.

During this period, we were also dealing with a family of bees on

our back deck. We thought they would go away on their own after I sprayed the nest, but they didn't. I had to have a pest control company come over, and they indicated it could take a few weeks for the "bumble" bees to buzz away. They finally did.

During this time frame, Barbara was wearing a heart monitor for a month to check her heart rhythms. The monitor would constantly get data readings and transmit them via the cell phone provided 24 hours a day. The monitor was connected to her chest and would occasionally seem that it wasn't working. We were assured that this is normal and part of the process, although Barbara would get frustrated with it as well. Just so you know, all the readings were normal, and she returned it on Sat, July 19, 2025.

I would like to tell you about a good deed that I did.

On Wed, July 09, 2025, I needed to go and pick up some copy paper at the local store. After I made my purchase, I left the store and proceeded to go to my car. Along the way, I noticed some small photos scattered around. I bent over to pick them up and noticed some more. I looked under a few cars and also found a bank book with last entry from 1957, a driver's license, an insurance card, and numerous other documents along with a military identification card from the Korean War time frame.

I immediately called Barbara and told her of my find and what my plan of action was. She said that I was the right man for the job.

The first thing I noticed was an address in Cranston on the bank book which obviously matched the name of the military ID which was dated 1952.

I GPS'd the directions, and to my surprise, the street in Edgewood in Cranston was only a few blocks away from where Barbara grew up. I drove up to the house and noticed it was a large Victorian house. I rang the doorbell, and no one answered. I left a written note and one of the documents and asked them to get in touch with me. It has been more than two weeks, so I assume I will not be hearing back from them. I also went online to the website that shows who owns homes, and it gave me a totally different name than what was on the military ID.

I wasn't discouraged since I never give up. As many of you know, I can be a pain in the ass, and I never give up, and I was determined to find out who belongs to the documents that I found. I thought that it could be highly likely the man could be deceased since he was in the Korean War. I made the assumption since if he was a soldier from age 18 and today it's 2025, he would most likely be around 93 years old.

I then went online and searched funeral home records in RI and found many names similar to his, but none with his first name. I did, however, find an obituary with his last name, and it mentioned some relatives who had passed away in New Hampshire a few years ago. I contacted numerous funeral homes in New Hampshire and told them my story. The first three told me that they couldn't help me, but the fourth said he would do some research and get back in touch with me. A few minutes later, he called me back and told me that the man in question had indeed died and that he had a living relative in Warwick, RI. He would reach out to the relative and give him my contact information. Five minutes later, I received a call from the man's nephew, who told me that he believed he knew what had happened. The nephew was cleaning out his late uncle's home and had found 40-50 boxes of documents, which he had taken to a store in Cranston to shred. He believed a few documents had fallen out of the box in the parking lot, and that is how I found them.

He told me he wanted to come over to my house immediately to retrieve them, to which I replied, "Of course." A short while later, he came to my house, shook my hand, and said he was very happy that I had gotten in touch with him. He started looking at the documents and told me the only thing he would keep was the military ID, and everything else would be shredded.

The final funny thing to the story is that I asked the man what he did, and he said he had been an attorney for many years. When I asked him where, he told me at a large company in RI that my relative was the chief information officer for many years. And as we say in Rhode Island, "It's not what you know, but who you know."

On Sat, Aug 09, 2025, our granddaughter Maya came over and spent time with us at a cookout we were having. While chatting with her, she told us that the night before, at around 12:30 a.m., she had seen a rather large spider crawling on the wall of her bedroom. I asked what she did to get rid of the spider. She responded like every other 13-year-old teenager living in today's high-priced and fast-forwarding life that we all live. She said, "I called Dad, whose room is next door, but he didn't respond." I asked why not, and with a small grin and chuckle, she replied, "He didn't answer his cell phone." I guess I finally realize that this is life today, no more and no less.

Many other incidents happened to me over the next few months,

but rather than bore you reading them, I will conclude with a funny one that was on Thanksgiving, Nov 27, 2025.

Barbara had decided early that morning to finish cooking the turkey, stuffing, and all the fixings that people love to partake of on this holiday. She was tired but decided to go to the YMCA nearby to participate in her Zumba class. Before leaving the house, she put a soap pod in the dishwasher and turned it on so that we would have enough clean dishes when all our guests would arrive for dinner at 2:00 p.m.

She left the house, and within a few short minutes, there was a huge amount of soap suds pouring out all over the kitchen floor. I immediately called her, and she said she would turn around and come home.

I ran down to the basement and brought up my shop vac so I could first drain all the water out of the dishwasher and also suck up all the soap suds all over the kitchen floor. I filled up the bucket four times before I accomplished the mission.

When Barbara arrived, she realized that she put a washing machine pod in rather than a dishwasher pod. This resulted in the huge amount of bubbles.

She told me it reminded her of the time her late father, Sumner Gold, did the same thing many years ago.

We laughed a little and joked and thought it could have been worse had we not been home to clean up the mess.

I guess you can say we did have the cleanest kitchen floor that day and that Barbara kept up the family tradition: "Bubbles, Bubbles down the drain."

I am done patting myself on the back, and I assume that you are as well.

The Spelling of the Word G-D

You may wonder why throughout the book I spell the word G-D instead of the most common spelling with three letters. Some people of the Jewish faith believe that this is a sign of respect and comes from an interpretation of the commandment in Deuteronomy 12:4 regarding the erasing, destroying, or desecrating the name of G-D. Writing "G-d" instead of spelling out the three letters is a fairly recent custom in America. Many believe this to be a sign of respect; according to the medieval commentator Rishi, we should not erase or destroy G-d's name and should avoid writing it.

Conclusion

A few thoughts for the reader to contemplate:

You can't do anything about the length of your life, but you can do something about its width and depth (author unknown).

A matter of perspective.

We ourselves feel that what we're doing is just a drop in the ocean, but the ocean would be less because of that missing drop (Author: Mother Teresa).

Wisdom begins in wonder (Socrates).

Some of you reading my book will probably realize that what you're going to be reading in the next numerous pages seems to be a repeat from a prior book, and you are correct. If you want to skip ahead, feel free to do so. My thoughts haven't changed that much, and that is the reason I repeat some of them in the book you are now reading. The only things that have changed are that I have gotten a year older, a little skinnier, a little smarter, but I remain the fun-loving, sensitive, caring husband, father, and friend who still is, of course, handsome as ever.

This book that you are reading is called *Would You Believe*. I guess you could say it's a continuation of my four prior books that have been published. Telling these additional stories has been a tremendous emotional release for me, and I'm glad that I finally got it done, although it took a lifetime of living to be able to tell my stories.

Barbara has always told me that with all the hardships and family deaths in my life, I needed a therapist. I guess she was right. Writing these books has been and always will be my therapy. She has always told me that I should forgive and forget friends and relatives who I believe have transgressed against me. To be honest, I have always had a hard time doing just that. Sometimes I blame myself for my son Max's death. I question myself if I did the right thing, if I made the correct medical decisions or not. In reality, everything we do and every decision that one makes is all in G-D's hands.

The world that we are leaving to our children and grandchildren is all messed up, in my own humble opinion. It's not too late to change if we all try to make the planet a better place to live.

I had attempted to write a summary of my life and the way that I have lived, but in the end, I decided that my short stories told it all. In conclusion, I simply say, thank you for reading my book. I told the truth, and perhaps someday the reader may also choose to put pen to paper. None of us know when the clock of life will run out for all of us. So, for me, no time like the present seemed the correct time and place to tell my stories.

Acknowledgments

My wife of 45-plus years, Barbara, stood by me during the process of writing this book and always offered kind words and understanding, even when I drove her crazy at times. I always appreciate her witticisms and constructive criticism whenever they are presented to me. To be able to have someone to love me during all of our times together, whether they be good or bad, is truly a blessing. I can't thank her enough for always standing by my side, and I will always cherish her counsel, love, and understanding.

I also need to mention my late son, Max, who passed away at the young age of 20 on Feb 18, 2004. He dedicated his short life to helping those in need. May his memory always be a blessing.

About the Author

Kevin Dwares is now a five-time author, writing this book about his ongoing life experiences. This book, called "Would You Believe," is published by Stillwater River Publications located in West Warwick, Rhode Island. It took many months to complete and consists of numerous short, true stories of his life from his birth on Oct 28, 1955, and is a continuation and culmination of his four prior books.

Kevin's fourth book, entitled "Right Place, Right Time Part 2," was published by Stillwater River Publications located in West Warwick, RI.

Kevin's third book, entitled "Right Place, Right Time," was published by Stillwater River Publications located in West Warwick, Rhode Island. This book took fifteen months to complete and consists of fifty-four short, true stories of his life from his birth on Oct 28, 1955, until the time of the publication of the book. The stories are accurate and truthful, and they have a humorous side as well.

Kevin's second book, entitled "A Royal Crowning Achievement," was published by Stillwater River Publishing in 2003, located in Pawtucket, Rhode Island. This book took nine months to complete and is about his dental experiences from 2020-2022 when he had 14 dental crowns placed in his mouth. The book details his 45 appointments and also has a humorous side to the story.

Kevin wrote his first book, entitled "Live to the Max," which was published in 2016 by the Christian Faith Publishing Company and took fifteen years to complete due to the sensitivity of the subject matter. This book is about the life and faith of his late son, Max Gold Dwares, who passed away on Feb 18, 2004, at the age of twenty from complications related to a bone marrow transplant to cure him of Leukemia.

Prior to writing his first book, Kevin spent over thirty years as a federal employee doing what he does best. He was loyal and trustworthy, and when he retired, he was offered two possible scenarios if he ever publicly discussed his career. He was offered #1, a FPC (Federal Prison Cell), or #2, DD (and I don't mean Dunkin' Donuts) but DD (Direct Deposit) of his pension check, and you can figure out what I chose to accept.

During his spare time, he likes to walk, go to flea markets and craft fairs, exercise, and spend time traveling around the United States and Israel, which he has visited nine times. Kevin spends time volunteering at food pantries and collecting donations to distribute to local organizations to distribute to the needy.

Kevin also volunteers at Rhode Island T.F. Green International Airport in Warwick, RI.

Kevin also volunteered at the Tomorrow Fund for Children with Cancer and has decided once again to donate all proceeds from the sale of "Would You Believe" to The Tomorrow Fund to help children and their families! Feel free to make a donation to them at:

The Tomorrow Fund
RI Hospital Campus
110 Lockwood Street
Physician's Office Bldg.
Suite 422
Providence, RI 02903
401.444.8811
www.tomorrowfund.org

Kevin lives in Cranston, Rhode Island, with his wife of 45 years, Barbara, his dog Harry, and his cat named Gaby. Kevin's son Jake and his wife Maria and daughter Maya live less than five minutes away. Kevin hopes that this new book will serve as an inspiration to others who have gone through many personnel experiences, some good and some bad, but are unable to discuss them for various reasons. As always,

Kevin leaves you with the comments. Remember, life is for the living, so always Live to the Max (L'chaim).

I will leave you with the following few cartoon pictures that I believe sum up my book and that you can all relate to:

www.ingramcontent.com/pod-product-compliance
Lightning Source LLC
LaVergne TN
LVHW010838120826
845149LV00017B/3306

* 9 7 8 1 9 6 8 5 4 8 4 6 9 *